# THE NEW EVANGELIZATION

By the same author from Mondadori

*Nel mondo dei credenti*

*Identità dissolta*

# THE NEW EVANGELIZATION

## RESPONDING TO THE CHALLENGE OF INDIFFERENCE

RINO FISICHELLA

GRACEWING

*La nuova evangelizzazione*
First published in 2011
in the Collezione Saggi
by Arnoldo Mondadori Editore SpA, Milano

First published in English in 2012 by
Gracewing
2 Southern Avenue
Leominster
Herefordshire HR6 0QF
United Kingdom
www.gracewing.co.uk

Published in Australia by
Freedom Publishing Pty Ltd
35 Whitehorse Road
Balwyn
Victoria 3103

English translation by Very Rev G. J. Woodall
The Scripture citations are taken from *The Jerusalem Bible*

ISBN 978 085244 796 3

Typeset by Gracewing

Cover design by Bernardita Peña Hurtado

# CONTENTS

# CHAPTER 1

# A CHALLENGE

## Recalling history

When I met Benedict XVI in a private audience on 29th March 2010, I knew nothing of the conversation he would have with me. Every meeting I had had with him, and also my numerous meetings previously with John Paul II, had been regulated by a work schedule and the contents of the conversations had been known in advance in order to be able to arrive prepared. On this occasion, however, everything was arranged in a rather unusual way. Monsignor Georg Gänswein, who had informed me in advance of the audience, had maintained an enigmatic reserve. My repeated and insistent attempts to discover more only produced the effect of yet another mysterious phrase: 'The Holy Father wants to speak to you about an assignment *auf der Leib geschneidert*'.[1] He used the German expression to help me better to understand the concept. Nevertheless, the clarity of the image did not in fact put me at ease. I was thumbing the pages of the *Annuario Pontificio* to try to understand what 'made to measure' might mean for me, but I found nothing; or, to put it better, I saw that I would have to adapt myself to a number of possible assignments.

Notwithstanding my allergy to 'rumours' which often may be heard on the occasion of transfers, I tried to follow the various opinions which were already being presented to me as certain in some of the congregations. Past experience, however, had already convinced me that what was said in the morning was no longer valid by evening.

'Rumours' are a sport which is widely practised in some quarters and the race to know ahead of time which appointments are being made must provide some people with thrilling emotions which, by contrast, leave me completely indifferent. For this reason, in the end, in the weeks prior to the conversation, I thought only of continuing my daily work, awaiting with patience and serenity the audience with the Holy Father.

I would never have thought, seated in front of a smiling Benedict XVI, almost taking pleasure in the situation, that he might say to me, literally: 'I have been thinking a great deal in these recent months. I wish to establish a dicastery for the new evangelization and I am asking you to be its president. I will let you have some of my notes. What do you think?' I was very surprised; I was only able to say: 'Holy Father, it is a great challenge.' The conversation proceeded with an exchange of considerations related to this project, to the point of sketching out the structure of the new dicastery. I left the audience very pleased. The fear I had felt up to half an hour before was changed into enthusiasm. Besides, I have spent the last thirty years of my life studying, teaching and writing about how to present Christianity to the people of today, how to stimulate reflection on the love of Jesus Christ, dead and risen, how to reconcile faith and reason to give strength and freedom to the act of faith … In the end, I thought, the Holy Father is putting me to the test; it is as if he had said: 'You have spent so much time studying; now let me see if it is all only theory…'

In the following days, reflecting upon my future service, I could not get rid of the thought of how the Lord had taken me by the hand through so many years just to bring me to this point. I looked back over my life and the connecting thread, which so many times I had tried in vain to pick out, all at once became clear. Everything had been leading me to this decisive point; to present to people of our time the need for faith in Jesus Christ.

If I have allowed myself this biographical diversion, it is only so that I may share a truth which seems to me it is important to recall in order better to understand the origin of events. The following pages are no more than a personal reading of how I see the new evangelization.

A few deadlines will help to bring the question more clearly into focus. First of all, in October 2012, the synod of bishops has been called to reflect upon the theme 'The new evangelization and witness to Christian faith'. Then, there is the apostolic exhortation from the Holy Father which will follow, in which also the considerations of the synod will be gathered and organised; in that exhortation a more organic, adequate and effective vision will be proposed to delineate the way the Church will be called to proceed in the decades which lie ahead. Taking into account these appointments and documents, what you will read in this book has no pretension to be other than a series of personal reflections on a theme which challenges the Church, especially in the West. The interest which the institution of the Pontifical Council for the New Evangelization has awakened in the world is truly extraordinary and the expectations which it has aroused show all the more the *prophetic* intuition of Benedict XVI. I use this expression intentionally, an expression which is strong in terms of its theological connotation. In fact, it intends to make us reflect first of all on the present of the Church. The here and now are not categories which are out of place; on the contrary, they oblige us to focus realistically upon the age in which we live in such a way that each one of us becomes aware of the weight of their own responsibilities. At the same time, however, it presses us to learn how to look to the future in a way which is far-sighted, so that this future does not find us unprepared or passive in the sense of being subjected to it, but capable of reacting to it in a way which is free, the result of a faith which remains alert and attentive. I hope, therefore, that the pages of this book may be able to help us understand the great challenge which awaits the Church in the decades to come, a challenge which it is not exaggerated to consider a challenge of our age.

As I shall attempt to show, the fact that we find ourselves at the end of an age that, for good or ill, has marked our history for almost six centuries forces us to take seriously the new one which lies on the horizon. We do not know yet with certainty what it involves. What can be established with certainty at present is only some pointers which orientate us towards a new epoch. As yet, it is difficult to be able to say who will be the protagonists of this period. What I consider important, in a period of transition like this one, is that the Church recognise her responsibility to take upon herself the task of transmitting a living patrimony of culture and of values which cannot be allowed to fall into oblivion. If that were to happen, the consequences would be damaging for the very civilisation which people wish to build up. It would be born blind and lame. It would be incapable of looking to the future and would be equally incapable of being able to build it. Only a living tradition, able to sustain and to consolidate the patrimony constructed across the centuries, is able to guarantee a future which is genuine.

This would not be the first time that the Church has undertaken this task. Our history provides evidence of the role which she has been able to fulfil at times of cultural crisis and of momentous change. Without wishing to repeat the salient givens of history, it suffices to look at the fourth century to understand with what great care the Christian community, led by bishops of intelligence, courageous and wise, knew how to navigate through the channel between the crisis of the Roman Empire and the emergence of Christian culture. The same can be said of the dawn of humanism and of the Renaissance, when far-sighted Popes glimpsed the genius of Michelangelo, Raphael, Titian, Tasso … and threw open to them the doors which allow us also to enjoy the treasures of art which they brought into being, and not without enormous sacrifices. True, there were also 'dark' moments; unfortunately, history is not a parable of growth so much as a sinusoid which reveals inevitably high points and low points which are the fruit of the very nature of human beings.

## Prophetic intuition

The decision of Benedict XVI to institute the Pontifical Council for the Promotion of the New Evangelization became official during the celebration of First Vespers of the solemnity of Saints Peter and Paul. In the basilica of St Paul's outside the walls, during the homily, he stated:

> I have decided to create a new organ, in the form of a Pontifical Council, whose principal task will be the promotion of a renewed evangelization in countries where the first announcement of the Gospel has already been sounded and where Churches of ancient foundation are already present, but which are experiencing a progressive secularisation of society and a kind of 'eclipse of the sense of God', which constitute a challenge as to how to find means which are adequate to propose anew the perennial truth of the Gospel of Christ.

The official birth of the new dicastery, by means of the apostolic letter, *Ubicumque et semper* bears the date of the 21st September 2010, the liturgical feast of the apostle and evangelist, St Matthew. The choice of date is symbolic and points to something of great significance: the new evangelization is in strict continuity with the command of Jesus to send his apostles into the whole world and this new mandate finds its fundamental point of reference in the Gospel. I think that the foundation of this new Council can be considered 'prophetic'. As already noted, I use the adjective intentionally because in this way the need to look at the present is qualified by the intention of giving a response to the great challenges which it poses; however, the regard we have is at the same time a far-sighted one because it obliges us to look to the future to understand in what way the Church will be called to exercise its ministry

in a world which is exposed to major cultural transforma-
tions which mark out the beginning of a new age for
humanity. By means of this prophetic announcement,
therefore, the Pope wishes to imbue the missionary spirit
of the Church with new force, especially in those places in
which the faith seems to be weakened under the pressure
of secularism.

This thought emerges clearly from the apostolic letter,
*Ubicumque et semper*, in which Benedict XVI writes:

> In our own time one of the particular features (of the
> Church's mission) has been to face up to the phe-
> nomenon of people distancing themselves from the
> faith, which has manifested itself progressively in
> societies and in cultures which for centuries
> appeared to have been imbued by the Gospel. The
> social transformations which we have seen in recent
> decades are the product of complex causes whose
> roots stretch back over a long period of time and
> which have altered profoundly our perception of the
> world. We only have to think of the enormous
> progress in science and technology, of the expansion
> of life-expectancy and in the possibilities there are
> for individual freedom, of the profound changes in
> the field of economics, of the changes brought about
> by the encounters of ethnic and cultural groups
> brought about by mass immigration, of the increas-
> ing inter-dependence between peoples. All of this
> has not been without consequences also for the
> religious dimension of human life. If, on the one
> hand, humanity has derived undeniable benefits
> from such transformations and if the Church has
> received from it further stimuli to render witness to
> the hope that she bears (cf. 1 Pt 3:15), on the other
> hand a worrying loss of the sense of the sacred has
> been experienced, which has gone to the point of
> calling into question those very foundations which
> once seemed to be beyond question, such as faith in
> God as creator and as providence, the revelation of
> Jesus Christ as the one and only saviour and our
> common understanding of fundamental human

experiences such as birth, death, living in a family, and the reference to a natural moral law.[2]

In a way which is even more direct he delineates the areas of competence to which the new evangelization must principally be dedicated:

> Taking upon myself the concerns of my venerable predecessors, I consider it appropriate to offer some answers sufficient for the Church as a whole, allowing herself to be regenerated by the power of the Holy Spirit, to present herself to the contemporary world with a missionary zeal capable of promoting a new evangelization. This refers above all to Churches of ancient foundation, which, while living through realities which are significantly different from one another and which have correspondingly different needs, require different impulses for evangelization. In some territories, in fact, even in the face of the progress of the phenomenon of secularisation, Christian practice still shows itself to be a thriving reality and to be profoundly rooted in the soul of entire populations, but, in other regions, a more evident distancing of society as a whole from the faith can be noted, together with a weaker ecclesial fabric, even if it is not deprived of elements of vivacity which the Holy Spirit does not fail to arouse. Unfortunately, we are aware also of some areas which appear to be almost completely de-Christianised, in which the light of the faith is entrusted to the witness of small communities; these communities, which need a renewed initial proclamation of the Gospel, seem to be particularly resistant to many aspects of the Christian message. The diversity of these situations requires careful discernment; talk of 'new evangelization, in fact, does not mean that it is necessary to produce a single formula, the same for all circumstances. Nevertheless, it is not difficult to recognise that what all the Churches living in areas which have been traditionally Christian need is a renewed missionary drive, the expression of a new and generous openness to the gift of grace.[3]

## *A fruit of Vatican II*

The institution of the Pontifical Council for the New Evangelization has its roots in a soil which is rich, by which it is sustained and which allows it to find a foundation which is solid, as well as the orientation for its future commitment. I am convinced that this dicastery represents one of the more mature fruits of Vatican II. At a distance of already fifty years from the opening of that Council, it is necessary to return to the words of John XXIII to recall the aims of Vatican II. In his programmatic allocution, *Gaudet Mater Ecclesia*, he made a number of references to the capacity to look at our contemporary world in its changed relationship with God to rediscover ways which may prove adequate for enabling it to understand the Gospel. The strongest expression of this theologically is, probably, also the most well known:

> It is necessary that doctrine itself be examined more broadly and more deeply and that people drink of it and be informed of it more fully, something desired by all who sincerely proclaim Christian, Catholic and Apostolic truth. It is necessary that this doctrine, certain and immutable, and to which faithful assent must be given, be deepened and expounded in a way which is demanded by our age. In fact, the deposit of faith is one thing, that is to say the truths which are contained in our venerable doctrine, but the way in which they are expressed is another, always, though, with the same meaning and the same understanding.[4]

*Distinction between Content & Form*

A number of times in the same speech, the Pope referred to concepts which can be related to the theme of the new evangelization. He spoke of 'strength of new energies', 'a new order of things', 'looking at the present, which has brought about new situations and new ways of living and which has opened up new avenues for the Catholic apostolate', 'we must not just safeguard this precious treasure, as if we were only concerned with what is ancient, but, at the ready, without fear, we must continue in the work which our age requires of us, following the path which the Church has pursued for almost twenty centuries'. All these expressions are signs of a far-sightedness, which recognized new ways of proclaiming the Gospel which is the same for ever.

There could be much discussion about what Vatican II meant for the recent history of the Church; however, from whichever angle it is examined, it continues to follow the objective of seeking to put the Church on the main road to the evangelization of the contemporary world. Both *Lumen gentium* and *Gaudium et spes*, to refer to the two most ecclesiological constitutions, but also *Sacrosanctum concilium* and *Dei Verbum*, do nothing other than express the same basic idea with its implied problematic, that is how to carry out its principal mission and it priority mission of proclaiming the Gospel in a way which is renewed and effective.

One important point of reference, though, can be to certain texts in which the Council explicitly declares this requirement, which today we recognise under the denomination 'the new evangelization'. One which will serve for all is that found in the decree on the Church's missionary activity, *Ad gentes*:

> This task (of evangelization) is one and unchangeable in every place and in every situation, even if, on the basis of the variety of different circumstances, it is not carried out in the same way. These differences, then, while they are to be kept in mind in these activities of the Church, are not born of the intrinsic nature of its mission, but stem only from the circumstances in which that one mission is carried out. Those conditions depend both on the Church and on peoples, human groups or the people to whom that mission is directed. In fact, the Church, even though it possesses, in a way which is full and complete, the means which are suitable for salvation, neither acts nor can act always and immediately in a way which is complete. In her action which moves towards the realisation of the divine plan, she recognises beginnings and

degrees; yet, sometimes, after happy beginnings, she
has to acknowledge regrettably a reversal or at least
she finds herself in a state of inadequacy and of
insufficiency ... To whatever condition or stage she
finds herself, her acts need to correspond in a way
which is appropriate and the instruments she uses
need to be adequate ... In this missionary activity of
the Church different conditions are to be found and
often mixed with one another; first there is the beginning or the foundation and then the new development
or period of youth. Yet, even when these phases have
been concluded, the missionary activity of the Church
does not cease; it is then the turn of the particular
Churches which are already organised to continue it,
preaching the Gospel to all those who are still outside
it. Besides, the human groups among whom the
Church finds herself change radically for various
reasons, out of which there can arise completely new
situations. In this case, the Church has to evaluate
whether these are such as to require once more her
missionary activity.[5]

As may be observed even from this last phrase, Vatican II's
perspective is put forward, concerning the need to develop
a new way in which the Church may fulfil what she is called
by her nature to do, to conduct evangelization.

About ten years later, Paul VI called together the synod
of bishops on the theme of evangelization and his apostolic
exhortation, *Evangelii nuntiandi* (1975) preserves its relevance intact. The Pope echoed and confirmed the words of
John XXIII:

On this tenth anniversary of the closing of the
Second Vatican Council, whose objectives may be
summed up in the end in one alone: to make the
Church in the twentieth century more suitable for
proclaiming the Gospel to human beings of the
twentieth century..., it is absolutely necessary to
place our selves before a patrimony of faith which
the Church has the duty to preserve in its intangible
purity, but also to present to people of our time, as

far as is possible, in a way which is comprehensible and persuasive.[6]

We do not find in the exhortation the expression "new evangelization"; even so, it speaks concretely of a new way of proclaiming the Gospel. Those pages, amongst other things, are an impressive analysis of the changes which had taken place in the world, affected by the phenomenon of generalised contestation. The Council, for reasons of time, had not even had the opportunity to take note of this fact, but in the synod these problems were very much present, just as there emerged with great clarity the Church's desire to rediscover the high road of mission, even if the bishops had not found complete agreement as to the ways in which this was to be realised.

Paul VI's expression: 'The rupture between the Gospel and culture is certainly the drama of our age, as it was also of other times';[7] if on the one hand it reveals the core of the problem, on the other it remains a source of provocation, after decades spent reflecting upon the matter, especially in the light of another expression typical of Pope Montini, an expression taken up by Benedict XVI in *Caritas in veritate*, according to which: 'The world is suffering from a lack of thought'.[8] Certainly, Paul VI recalled forcefully that:

> The Gospel and therefore evangelization, are not identifiable with culture and are independent with respect to all cultures. Nevertheless, the kingdom which the Gospel announces is lived out by people profoundly attached to a culture and the building up of the kingdom cannot but make use of culture and of human cultures. While they remain independent of cultures the Gospel and evangelization are not necessarily incompatible with these, but are capable of penetrating into all cultures without becoming the servant of any of them.[9]

For this reason and without rhetoric, he claimed: 'We must evangelize culture and human cultures, not in a decorative sense in a way similar to superficial panting, but in a way which is alive, profound and reaching the roots, in the rich and broad meaning that these words have in the Constitution *Gaudium et spes*, starting always from the person and returning always to relationships of persons with one another and with God.'[10]

Certainly, the Pope was aware that the action of evangelising is complex and the risk of making one part of it absolute would have led to obscuring the mission itself; for this reason, wisely, he recalled the fact that: 'No definition which is partial and fragmentary can provide a sufficient explanation of the rich, complex and dynamic reality which is that of evangelization, without running the risk of impoverishing and in the end of mutilating it. It is impossible to understand evangelization unless we try to embrace all the essential parts which constitute it.'[11] However, he affirmed forcefully and without leaving room for equivocation: 'There is no real evangelization unless the name, the teaching, the life, the promises, the kingdom, the mystery of Jesus of Nazareth, Son of God, are proclaimed'.[12]

Nevertheless, Paul VI's genuine concern that evangelization should be something new is to be found once more explicitly in this passage:

> This problem of 'how to evangelize' always remains a current question because the methods vary according to the circumstances of time, of place, of culture and, as such, throw up a certain challenge to our capacity for discovery and for adaptation. Upon us especially, Pastors of the Church, falls the responsibility for recreating, boldly, wisely and in complete fidelity to its content, the most appropriate and effective ways of communicating the Gospel message to the people of our time.[13]

He recalls some points which remain valid as elements of fundamental content for the new evangelization today: the liturgy, the primacy of witness, the need to obtain instruction in using the new instruments of social communication, popular piety…; in fact, the relevance of *Evangelii nuntiandi* is not in dispute and its conclusion provides us with a constant challenge:

> Therefore, we exhort our brothers in the episcopacy, placed in that position by the Holy Spirit to govern the Church. We exhort priests and deacons, collaborators of the bishops in gathering the People of God and in the spiritual animation of the local communities. We exhort the religious, witnesses to a Church called to sanctity and thus themselves participants in a life which expresses the beatitudes of the Gospel. We exhort lay people, Christian families, young people and adults, those involved in the professions, managers, without forgetting the poor so often rich in faith and hope, all lay people conscious of their role in evangelization in the service of the Church or in the midst of society and of the world. We say to all: it is necessary that our zeal for evangelization stem from true sanctity of life and, as the Second Vatican Council reminds us, that preaching, fed by prayer and especially by the love of the Eucharist, may in its turn cause to grow in holiness the one who preaches. The world which, despite numerous signs of the rejection of God, paradoxically searches for him through unexpected paths and which feels its need of him in times of sorrow, asks for evangelizers who may speak to this world of a God whom they may come to know and with whom they are familiar, as if they were able to see him who is invisible. The world requires and expects of us simplicity of life, a spirit of prayer, charity towards all and especially towards the little ones and the poor, obedience and humility, self-detachment and sacrifice. Without this sign of holiness, our word will find it difficult to open up the way to the hearts of the people of our time, but will risk being vain and fruitless.[14]

John Paul II, with the strength of his magisterium introduced the formula 'the new evangelization'. It is difficult to know whether the Pope succeeded in imagining fully the very real movement that would be created subsequently to these words; even so, in its ambiguity, it pointed out generally the path to be followed and in the various forms of pastoral work found a happy acceptance. From this time on, in fact, so many realities in the Church understood that their actions had to be directed towards this horizon. Many understood its urgency and applied to themselves the words of Paul: 'It (preaching the Gospel) is a duty which has been laid on me; I should be punished if I did not preach it' (1 Cor 9:16) and they brought enthusiasm and power into places where weariness and confusion had insinuated themselves. Hence, the question of evangelization, on the one hand, reveals a basic nucleus with which the Church has to take account in the course of the centuries because this constitutes part of her very nature; on the other hand, it demonstrates that the solutions repeatedly put forward in recent decades, however good and valuable the proposals advanced may have appeared, are even so inadequate and a renewed commitment is required which involves the Church in the first person.

## Notes

[1]   Translator's note: 'made to measure'.

[2]   Benedict XVI, *Ubicumque et semper*, preamble.

[3]   *Ibid.*

[4]   John XXIII, *Gaudet Mater Ecclesia*, n. 6.5.

[5]   Second Vatican Council, *Ad gentes*, n. 6.

[6]   Paul VI, *Evangelii nuntiandi*, nn. 2-3.

[7]   *Ibid.*, n. 20.

[8]   Benedict XVI, *Caritas in veritate*, n. 53.

[9]   Paul VI, *Evangelii nuntiandi*, n. 20.

[10]   *Ibid.*

[11]   *Ibid.*, n. 17.

[12]   *Ibid.*, n. 22.

[13]   *Ibid.*, n. 40.

[14]   *Ibid.*, n. 76.

# CHAPTER 2

# THE NEW EVANGELIZATION

## *The foundation*

The New Testament uses a whole series of expressions to describe Jesus' activity of revelation; apart from that of 'proclaiming' or 'teaching', a word which recurs frequently to indicate his work is 'evangelising'. According to its normal meaning, already to be found in the Old Testament, this expresses the idea of announcing a message of joy, for example upon the birth of a child or after victory in battle. The meaning of the term, however, began to assume a significance which was more typically religious in the book of the prophet Isaiah. There we find these words written: 'How beautiful on the mountains are the feet of one who brings good news, who heralds peace, brings happiness, proclaims salvation and tells Zion: "Your God reigns" ' (Is 52:7). The reference in this verse is to the herald who goes ahead of the people returning from slavery in Babylon. The inhabitants of Jerusalem, who are to be found on the walls and on the turrets of the city, are waiting for the remnant and from the top of the mountain they spot the messenger who, shouting at the top of his voice, proclaims its liberation and their return to their homeland. In the prophet's mind, however, the herald is announcing the real victory; this is not so much the return from exile so much as the fact that God is returning to dwell in Zion, giving birth to a new stage in history. The same concept is taken up again by the prophet in another passage, where he says: 'The spirit of the Lord has been given to me because the Lord has anointed me; he has sent me to bring good news to the poor' (Is 61:1).

The similarity between these expressions and those we find in the New Testament is very close and is impressive. In his preaching Jesus identifies himself with the messenger of expectant joy. In his person and in the signs he accomplishes, he allows us to see brought to fulfilment the promise of God to give life to a new era in history, that of his kingdom. After him, the apostles, Paul and the disciples are identified as messengers who bear a proclamation of salvation and of joy. In a famous passage of the letter to the Romans the apostle quotes, literally, the passage from Isaiah and applies it to all Christians who proclaim the Gospel: 'But, they will not ask his help unless they believe in him and they will not believe in him unless they have heard of him and they will not hear of him unless they get a preacher and they will not have a preacher unless one is sent, but, as Scripture says: "The footsteps of those who bring good news is a welcome sound" ' (Rom 10:14–15). It is interesting to note that, in this quotation of the prophet the apostle does not mention the mountains. The underlying significance of this helps us to understand the task of the new evangelizers; they have a mission which is destined for the whole world. In the book of the Acts of the Apostles, in fact, the Gospel is directly identified with the person of Jesus, the messiah long awaited and now come into our midst: 'They preached every day in the temple and in private houses and their proclamation of the Good News of Jesus Christ was never interrupted.' (Ac 5:42).

As we can see from these initial reflections, evangelising is simply to be equated with bearing the Gospel. However, there is an awareness, deeply rooted in the sacred texts, according to which the good news which Jesus announces is not a new doctrine, but rather is Jesus himself in his own person. As the content of his proclamation of joy, it is he himself who reveals the mystery of the Father's love. To sum it up, in his own person the fulfilment of everything and the beginning of a new phase in the life of men and women and of history are given. The time has now come; in his person God says everything which is fundamental and essential for us to come to know him. What is asked for now is faith, as the response of love towards him. Once the Gospel is proclaimed, in fact, it needs to be heard; from this perspective the teaching of the apostle, Paul is very incisive: '... as long as you persevere and stand firm on the solid base of the faith, never letting yourselves drift away from the hope promised by the Good News which you have heard' (Col 1:23). However, the Gospel does not bear witness only to historical facts, such as the preaching the death and the resurrection of the Lord Jesus, insofar as this is the event of salvation for all those who believe in him. Being the living Word of God, he is also an event which challenges people, penetrates into their lives, calling them to conversion and creating a community of faith, hope and love. Indeed, it is not just a simple word, but it is a creative force which brings about what it expresses; Saint Paul recalls this: the good news 'came to you not only as words, but as power and as the Holy Spirit and as utter conviction' (1 Thess 1:5). All those who receive the Gospel become missionaries so that the joy which has been communicated to them and which has transformed their lives may allow others, too, to encounter the same source of love and of salvation.[1]

## *Development.*

If the verb 'to evangelize' and the term 'Gospel' are to be found very frequently in the sacred texts and, as a result, are commonly found in our language, 'to evangelize' is, nevertheless, a term which arose only at a later stage. In all probability, it was Erasmus who first inserted into our language the derived term 'to evangelize', to designate what he considered to be a form of Lutheran fanaticism. As we know, Luther identified as the foundation stone of his teaching the Gospel alone, insofar as it was the proclamation of pardon and of salvation through faith in Jesus Christ. The Council of Trent, for its part, was constrained to intervene to maintain the broader understanding of the Catholic faith. Thus it was that misunderstanding gained the upper hand and, from the time of the Council of Trent, the Catholic world maintained a certain reluctance to use the verb 'to evangelize' because it held it to be too Protestant. It preferred, therefore, to speak of 'mission'. Only in the eighteenth century did some Protestants begin to understand the need for missionary activity, neglected at the beginning of the Reformation, and it was actually on that occasion that they began to make reference to the term 'evangelization', a circumstance which, obviously, became a further pretext for Catholics not to use the term.

In the end, also on our side, especially under the impact of the catechetical renewal of the 50s, we began to speak of 'evangelization', to distinguish it from catechesis and from other forms of pastoral activity. Therefore, we speak about evangelization as the activity of the Church which was identified with the first proclamation of the Gospel and of catechesis to define the systematic formation of believers who had already been evangelized. Since language at times follows the need for precision on the part of specialists, other expressions were introduced, for example 'pre-evangelization' to indicate the preparation of non-Christians for the explicit proclamation of the Gospel. If, on the one hand, this recourse to linguistic subtleties is useful for specifying a particular reality, unfortunately, it is not always useful for providing a clear vision of the whole.

One last rapid glance at the evolution of the use of terminology reveals an interesting fact. In the documents of the First Vatican Council (1869–1879), the term 'the Gospel' occurs only once, it is impossible to find the verb 'to evangelize' and, obviously, the term 'evangelization. In the documents of the Second Vatican Council,, on the other hand, 'Gospel' is used 157 times, 'to evangelize' 18 times and 'evangelization' 31 times.[2] As we know, the term came to assert itself more and more to the point of becoming part of our common language. The use of language, though, also points to an underlying culture and this leads us to identify the Church's activity of proclamation in the contemporary world as a priority.

## Genesis

It will not be without value now to examine the genesis of the expression 'the new evangelization'. The term appears for the first time, almost as a parenthesis, in the 1979 Puebla document. At the conclusion of the work of the Assembly, which had seen united together all the bishops of Latin America in this Mexican city, we find written in the final text:

> New situations, emerging from socio-cultural changes require a new evangelization: emigrants to other countries, large urban conglomerates in our own countries, masses from all levels of society in a precarious situation as to the faith, groups exposed to the influence of sects and of ideologies which do not respect their identity, causing confusion and provoking division.[3]

Some months later, during the visit to the Mogila sanctuary at Nova Huta, the same expression was used also for the first time by John Paul II. It was 9th June 1979, and Karol Wojtyla was returning to his own country of Poland as Pope. Nova Huta brings to mind the communist project of constructing an entire modern suburb, at the very gates of Cracow, where they were to make visible the power of that atheist ideology by means of the construction of the prototype of a communist city. The project placed at the heart of the area the great steel works, five times larger than the whole historic centre of Cracow, with wide avenues, broad spaces of green and dwellings for at least 40,000 workers, the same number as those who were to be taken on by the factory. The communist authorities did not intend even remotely to think of giving space for the building of a church. The then archbishop of Cracow, Karol Wojtyla, did not let himself become too upset. On Christmas night, 1973, in the freezing cold which is a characteristic of that land, he went to Nova Huta to celebrate Holy Mass in the open air. The influx of people was such that the authorities, civil and military, could not but go back on their decision not to permit the celebration. Returning to Nova Huta as Pope, John Paul II could not forget what had happened in the preceding years and how he himself had acted then in his own person so that, before the power of atheism and secularism, life might be given to a witness of living faith.

In the homily he preached on that occasion he proclaimed:

> Wherever the cross is raised up, there arises the sign that the Good News of the salvation of man through Love has already reached that place. Wherever the cross is raised up, there is the sign that evangelization has begun. Long ago our fathers raised up the cross, in various parts of the land of Poland, as a sign that already the Gospel had arrived, that that evangelization had begun which was to be extended without interruption up to our days. With this thought in mind, the first cross was also raised in Mogila, close to Cracow, close to Stara Huta. The new cross of wood was raised up not far from here, during the celebration of the millennium. With that cross we received a sign, that is to say that on the threshold of the new millennium, in these new times, in these new conditions of life, the Gospel is proclaimed once more. A new evangelization has begun, as if it were a question of a second proclamation, even though in reality it is always the same. The cross stands aloft above the world as it turns on its axis.

## New evangelization or re-evangelization?

From that time onwards, for twenty-seven years. John Paul II used this expression many times and in different settings. It is not a case here of going through each of these circumstances. A publication in the near future of the Pontifical Council over which I preside will show clearly the plurality of contexts and the differing nuances which the Pope applied to the expression from time to time. Still, it will not be without value to try to clarify two of John Paul's texts which appear to be in disagreement one with the other.

In 1983 at Haiti, speaking to the episcopal conference of Latin America on the importance of evangelization in those countries, he said:

> Looking today at the atlas of Latin America, with more than seven hundred dioceses, with insufficient but dedicated personnel, with its management and its structures, with its guidelines, with the moral authority which the Church enjoys, we have to recognise in all of this the fruit of centuries of patient and persevering evangelization. Almost five centuries; in fact, in 1992, already very close, there will occur the fifth centenary of the discovery of America and of the beginning of its evangelization. As Latin Americans, you must celebrate this date in the light of serious reflections about the paths trodden in the history of this part of the continent, but also with joy and pride. As Christians and as Catholics it is right to celebrate this occasion by looking at these five hundred years of work in proclaiming the Gospel and in building up the Church in these lands. Look to God in thanksgiving to him for the Christian and Catholic vocation of Latin America and of gratitude to those who were living and active instruments of evangelization. Look in fidelity to your past of faith. Look at the challenges of the present and at the efforts being made. Look to the future, to see how to consolidate the work which has been begun. The commemoration of the half-millennium of evangelization will have its full significance if there is a commitment on your part as bishops, together with your presbyterate and with your lay faithful, a commitment not to re-evangelization, but to a new evangelization. It will be new in its ardour, new in its methods and new in its expressions. In this

respect, allow me to entrust to you, synthesised in a
few words, the aspects which appear to me to be the
fundamental presuppositions for the new evangelization.[4]

The thinking of the Pope seems to be that of bringing out,
in the general context of the memorial of the five hundred
years of the first evangelization, that the Church must feel
the need for a renewed missionary enthusiasm, in such a
way as not to remain stuck in the past. The use of the triad
'ardour', 'methods' and 'expressions' confirms the interpretation of a renewed way of situating matters in regard to
the one and only evangelization undertaken by believers.
To sum it up, the Pope challenges the Churches of Latin
America so that they may be capable of renewing themselves, giving life to new and expressive forms of proclamation in a changed social context.

The second text in question is to found in the encyclical
*Redemptoris missio* (1990) where we read:

> The differences in activities within the one and only
> mission of the Church arise not from reasons intrinsic
> to the mission itself, but from the different circum-
> stances in which that mission is unfolded Looking at
> today's world from the point of view of evangeliza-
> tion, three situations can be distinguished. First of all,
> there is that to which the missionary activity of the
> Church is directed: peoples, human groups, socio-
> cultural contexts in which Christ and his Gospel are
> not known or in which Christian communities suffi-
> ciently mature to be able to incarnate the faith in their
> own setting and to announce it to other groups are
> lacking. This is the mission *ad gentes*, properly speak-
> ing. Then there are Christian communities which
> have adequate and solid ecclesial structures, are
> fervent in faith and in life, who irradiate the witness
> of the Gospel in their surroundings and who feel a
> commitment to the mission of the universal Church.
> Finally, there exists an intermediate situation, often
> in countries of ancient Christian tradition, but at times
> also in younger Churches, where entire groups of the

baptised have lost the living sense of the faith or even
no longer recognise themselves as members of the
Church, leading to an existence which is far from
Christ and from his Gospel. In this case there is need
for a 'new evangelization' or a 're-evangelization.[5]

The deliberate stress in the discourse in Haiti to affirm that
it was a case of a new evangelization and not of a re-
evangelization places a question mark over the inter-
changeability in the use of the two terms which are present
in the subsequent encyclical. Therefore we ask ourselves:
is the new evangelization a re-evangelization? The problem
lies in the prefix 're' and in the multiple meanings it can
have. It can express different meanings according to the use
to which it is put: it can indicate the repetition of an action,
as in the case of re-proposing something, but it can also
express the return to a prior phase and in an opposing sense
as in re-acquiring; in the same line of thought, it can also
have the sense of conferring new value to the verb from
which it is taken, as for example in 'to re-bind'. In our case,
what does re-evangelization seek to designate? The repetition of the evangelization which has always taken place?
Or a new evangelization in opposition to the preceding one?
It would be different and pejorative if the verb were used
in the third sense, that is of conferring something new value
in terms of content. In this jungle of interpretation, I
consider that it is best to avoid the neologism 're-evangelization', to allow us to speak of the new evangelization as a
form by means of which one and the same Gospel from the
beginning is proclaimed with new enthusiasm, in a new
language which is comprehensible in a different cultural
situation and with new methodologies which are capable
of transmitting its deepest sense, that sense which remains
immutable.

# Notes

1    For these considerations see G. Friedrich,«ευαγγελιξομαι», in *Grande Lessico del Nuovo Testamento* (GLNT), III, 1023-11-06.

2    Cf. A. Dulles, "John Paul II and the New Evangelization. What does it Mean?" in R. Martin — P. Williamson (ed), *John Paul II and the New Evangelization* (Cincinnati, 2006), p. 4.

3    Third General Conference of Latin American Bishops, *Puebla*, Final Document, chapter 2, 1.3, n. 366.

4    John Paul II, Discourse to the Assembly of Celam, Port-au-Prince, 9th March 1983.

5    Idem, *Redemptoris missio*, n. 33.

# CHAPTER 3

# THE CONTEXT

## *Secularism*

The preceding pages have recalled a number of times the fact that the need for a new evangelization is determined by the cultural and social context. For this reason we are obliged to take account of the theme of inculturation and of the effectiveness of the Gospel in terms of knowing how to insert itself into cultures, how to understand them, and how to form and transform them. In some respects this was easier in the past both when the Church undertook evangelization for the first time and when it entered along a collision path with ideologies. In fact, the point of reference was easily identifiable and, above all, it presented itself in a unitary form.

Today's context of fragmentation, the plurality of positions and especially the diversification of languages and of behaviours calls for a different approach and requires greater effort. Besides, at a time when we need to speak about the new evangelization of the West, the geographical extension of this reality presents a world which is not readily to be understood and that by reason of the variety of cultural traditions and languages involved. Therefore, we need to pay attention so that the analysis offered and the proposal advanced not be unduly weighted in favour of a European vision of reality. Hence, it is better to follow the path which allows us to identify the common denominator rather than to spend time seeking to underline differences.

One of the first themes which arises is the question of secularisation, which it seems best to treat on the basis of its more evident aspects. More than half a century has gone by since the 'manifesto' of modern secularisation emerged, re-worked and modified on the basis of the ideas of Dietrich Bonhoeffer, from Professor Harvey Cox of the American Baptist church in his book *The Secular City*. There followed almost immediately a second text, *Honest to God*, by the Anglican bishop of Woolwich, John A. T. Robinson. These two works made the public at large aware of the key ideas of a movement which had a broader horizon and much deeper roots than the direct influences we recognise in theology and in an ecclesial setting. The programme was focused upon the proclamation, now reduced to a technical formality: to live and to build up our world *etsi Deus non daretur*, as if God did not exist. The challenge was issued at the time upon a very fertile field and it was accepted enthusiastically, to the point where, today, at a distance of many years, we have to ask what degree of criticism was operative in those who accepted it or who went along with it. The Church had brought to a conclusion only shortly before this the Second Vatican Council and on the horizon the symptoms could already be glimpsed of a crisis which would engulf many believers, while the West was to experience a few years later the great contestation of its youth round about 1968. In short, many seemed to find in the ideas of secularisation the interpretative key to allow them to impress upon the world their drive for autonomy, and the Church seemed to find there the possibility of discovering the simplicity of its own origins. However, everything that glitters is not gold.

*Etiamsi daremus non esse Deum*. The affirmation of H. Grotius (1583–1645) was brought out into the open, but, looking at things more closely, the interpretations given to it went far beyond the intention of this Dutch expert in natural law. For this philosopher, in fact, what mattered was to show that there was a foundation for natural law, which, of its own very nature, retained its full value to such a point that it could survive the divisions between Christians. However, little by little, from the simple proclamation of a theoretical principle, and in some respects having positive elements insofar as it was directed towards a faith which would be mature and responsible, secularisation was transformed into secularism. The latter has infiltrated into institutions to such an extent that today it has become the culture and inspires the behaviour of masses of people, so much so that it is no longer possible to see any objective limits to it. However, as with any phenomenon, even secularisation cannot escape the ambiguity of its various aspects and the plurality of possible interpretations. It is difficult to specify the true role of Dietrich Bonhoeffer in this movement and it is very much more difficult to identify the effective meaning of his manifesto in the *Letters*:

> We must recognise honestly that we have to live in the world as if there were no God, and it is this that we really do recognise precisely before God. God himself leads us to this awareness; he makes us realise that we must live as human beings who are able to keep going forward without him. The God who is with us is the God who abandons us (Mk 15:34)! We are continually in the presence of the God who makes us live in the world without the hypothesis of God'.[1]

In the face of currents of thought founded upon concepts as generic and as utopian as these, it was not long before dubious and extremist versions made themselves felt; as has been said, secularisation degenerated into secularism, with negative consequences especially for the way we understand our existence as persons. In fact, secularism means separation from the Christian religion; the latter does not have and may not have any voice when we speak of our private lives or of public or social life. In short, our lives as persons are constructed by withdrawing from the horizon of religion, which is relegated to a simply private sphere, without any involvement in interpersonal, social or civic relations. Besides, within the private sphere, religion has its place, but it is a very restricted place; in fact, it intervenes only to a certain extent and marginally in regard to ethical judgments and behaviour.

At this point, to say that secularism is a phenomenon which is religiously neutral means not to recognise the consequences which have been visibly manifested in recent decades. However we may wish to judge the autonomy of the human being, this cannot ever be detached from its original link to the creator; cutting the umbilical cord cannot be equated to rejecting those who generated us. Creaturely autonomy has to be based upon the experience of gratuity, without which a coherent understanding of personal identity becomes impossible. Indeed, to reduce the whole process of secularisation to a critique of religious fanaticism or intolerance means to lose sight of the global nature of the movement and of the many faces under which it presents itself. Now that the enthusiasm of the seventies, which had gripped many people, has passed, it must be concluded that secularisation and secularism have been too hasty in the way they have identified God as a surrogate for life. From a contemporary perspective, however, in which a culture of death seems to overwhelm life itself, the fundamental theses of secularism, according to which this world has become 'adult' and, as a consequence, no longer has any need of God, still remain to be proven.

One of the first data to emerge from the project of secularism is the sporadic endeavour to attain complete autonomy. Contemporary human beings are characterised very strongly by jealousy for their own independence and for responsibility in their personal lives. Forgetful of every relationship with the transcendent, they have become allergic to all forms of speculative thought and limit themselves to a simple point in history, to a specific moment of time, and they delude themselves that only that is true which is the fruit of scientific verification. Once the relationship with the transcendental is lost and where every form of spiritual contemplation is rejected, they have fallen into a kind of empirical pragmatism, which induces them to hold an appreciation for facts but not for ideas. Without any kind of resistance, their mode of thought and their mode of life undergo rapid change, individuals become progressively ever more kinetic, that is to say always ready for some new experience, wanting to become involved in some new game even if it is greater than they are, especially if it finds them in that narcissism which is no longer concealed, but which deludes them as to the essence of life. Hence, the process of secularism has engendered an explosion of claims of individual liberty, which affect the sphere of sexual life, inter-personal and family relationships, activities undertaken in our free time, as also during working hours.

The realms of teaching and of communication have inevitably become involved in this and the whole context of life has been altered. However paradoxical it may seem, these social claims are always made in the name of justice and of equality, but at their root what is found to be determinative is the desire to live more freely at the individual level. More and more injustices and social inequalities are tolerated and in the end endured rather than permit prohibitions which may touch the private sphere. Thus, an entirely new situation has come to be established in which people want to replace older values, especially those expressed by Christianity. From a standpoint of this type, in which the human being has come to occupy the central ground, the barometer of every form of existence, God becomes a useless hypothesis and a competitor not only to be avoided, but to be eliminated. This radical change has taken place in a relatively easy fashion, the accomplices being often a weak theology and an approach to religion founded mostly upon sentiment and incapable of demonstrating the broader horizon of faith.

In this context God loses his central position. The consequence is that human beings lose their place. The 'eclipse' of the meaning of life reduces the person to the point of no longer knowing where he fits in, of not being able to find his place in the midst of creation and of society. In some ways we fall into the temptation of Prometheus; we delude ourselves into thinking we can become masters of life and of death, because we are the ones to decide when, how and where. A culture which tends to idolise the body, to be selective about interpersonal relationships on the basis of beauty and of physical perfection ends up by forgetting the essential. Thus, we fall constantly into a form of narcissism, which prevents us from rooting life in values which are permanent and solid and which limits us to what is ephemeral. For this reason, it is here that we find the great challenge for the future. Whoever wants to enjoy the liberty of living as though God did not exist can do so, but they should know what they are going to encounter. They should be aware that this choice is the premise neither for autonomy nor for liberty. Limiting ourselves to deciding what to do with our lives will never be able to satisfy the demand for freedom. Imposing silence upon the desire for God, which is rooted in our hearts, will never enable someone to achieve autonomy. The enigma of personal existence is not resolved by denying the mystery, but only by choosing to immerse ourselves in it. This is the path to follow; every short-cut risks causing us to lose ourselves in the meandering paths of a wood, from which it is impossible to see either the exit or the destination we seek to reach.

However much the reality of the present situation of permanent crisis in which the world finds itself may be able to challenge us to question ourselves, it has to be reiterated that this challenge is not primarily of an economic or financial order. If it were so, we could look to the future with relative calm because solutions, of an essentially technical nature, could be easily found. The crisis through which we are living is, first of all, a crisis of culture and, without going into too many details, we should add anthropological.[2] The human being is in crisis. We are no longer capable of finding ourselves, after having flattered ourselves that we were right especially when we had believed we had attained adulthood and had become complete masters of ourselves and independent of all authority. In fact, this song of the sirens was very enticing. To human beings ever more at the centre of things, sustained by a rediscovered narcissism which had been obscured for decades, incapable of finding the truth because deprived of all foundation, there remained one last block to becoming completely autonomous, the removal of God.

## Human beings disorientated

So, secularism has put forward the thesis of living in the world *etsi Deus non daretur*, as if God did not exist. Nevertheless, having removed God, our contemporaries have lost themselves. The desire to seek the face of God, which has always been the mark of an anxiety deep within the human heart, today has become weaker and the distancing of ourselves from God more evident. The only face reflected in our heart has become our own. That is too little, too little for us to define ourselves as adults, autonomous and independent. Reflecting our own face would have been able to satisfy the ever more dominant narcissism of our times,[3] but in the end it was discovered that, in those few square inches, sadness had the upper hand and the drama of life was re-presented with greater intensity. Yes, the drama of life, because it is a question of this. On his own, the human being dies before time does. Once we lose relationship with others, we cease to be *persons* and remain only individuals, each one a monad without any possibility of survival because a single individual is incapable of that love which generates life and solitude gains the upper hand. In this way the circle is closed, sadly, but unequivocally.

If God is relegated to a corner, the darkest and the furthest away from life, the human being becomes lost because there is no longer any meaning to being in relationship with oneself, much less with others. Therefore, it is necessary to bring God back to human beings of our time. If people do not wish to consider this proposal for reasons of a religious nature, it must be considered at least in order to restore a supply of oxygen to human beings who are gasping for breath, confused and more and more depressed. If our contemporaries wish to escape from the pathology which afflicts their lives and rediscover the place that is properly theirs, at the centre of things, they need to seek the face of God, impressed in that of his Son, made man, Jesus of Nazareth, who has revealed definitively its essential characteristics. On the face of that man is impressed the face of God (cf. Col 1:15). This is not to be found anywhere else; to find this, we must fix our gaze upon him. In some respects we return to Nazareth, into that synagogue where on the Sabbath day he used to go as a matter of custom to hear the word of the prophets. There not only did he give voice to the word proclaimed of old, but he proclaimed its fulfilment in his own person. 'The eyes of all were fixed on him' (Lk 4:20). In this way the evangelist expressed in broad terms the truth which was implied there. Probably, we would have to be capable of adopting the same expression if we want to bring about the *new* evangelization. In the synagogue he reveals himself as the evangelizer who brings salvation; for this reason we must keep our gaze fixed upon him.

## The West in crisis

Christianity was not born in Europe, but certainly Europe was born along with Christianity. We would need more ample space to be able to illustrate the truth of this simple affirmation. However, the historical truth expressed in this phrase will escape no-one. Christianity remains linked to the land rightly called 'Holy' because that land saw the realisation of the culminating point of every religious phenomenon, the incarnation of the Son of God. In him the revelation of God to mankind is brought about and is completed. From the time of Abraham, father of all those who give witness to faith in monotheism, history developed in that land in the light of the 'promise' and of the 'covenant', sign of the constant care of the part of God. As the apostle states: 'When the appointed time came, God sent his Son, born of a woman, born subject to the law, to redeem those subject to the law' (Gal 4:4). On the basis of this fact a new proclamation was made to human beings; once again, it is Paul who summarises this in the following words: 'There are no more distinctions between Jew and Greek, slave and free, male and female, but all of you are one in Christ Jesus' (Gal 3:28). In other words, the vision of humanity and of the world is changed. Faith in Jesus Christ destroys barriers because it touches us in our deepest reality. At his command, however, his disciples departed from that land, traversing the whole world, to proclaim to all his death and resurrection, as the seed of salvation for all who would believe in him. This is the given of history.

Nevertheless, it is equally a historical fact that Christianity developed and had its conceptual roots in those lands and in that thought which today we recognise as part of Europe. More than anyone else, Paul travelled these lands, proclaiming the Gospel. His journeys to Athens, Corinth, Thessalonica, the region of Galatia, Malta, Cyprus, Rome and Spain, give witness to the first presence of Christianity in our lands. In the philosophers of ancient Greece, the first Christian thinkers found the support necessary for explaining the mystery of faith and with those categories and that language they expressed the truth of the Gospel. Furthermore, the brilliant work of Leo the Great and his capacity, in the midst of the crisis of the Roman Empire, to enable the new populations, so-called 'barbarians', to understand the richness of the Roman tradition, to make it possible for this to live alongside their own cultures, and attaining a synthesis which had been previously unthinkable, was a work of great cultural and political significance, comparable in the succeeding centuries to the actions of Gregory the Great, who sent Benedictine monks as evangelizers everywhere, even to the point that they reached the Nordic countries. The same work was undertaken by the monks Cyril and

Methodius, whom Pope John VIII had sent in 880 to evangelize the lands to the east; they effected an incredible cultural achievement, even to the extent of inventing the alphabet which is still used there today. If we add this to the power drawn from the faith lived out by millions of pilgrims who, as they journeyed from one land to another, created the presuppositions for the exchange of cultures, traditions and different technologies, then we appreciate how much history makes it possible for us to know through the passing of the centuries.

Christianity has formed Europe, implanting into her that sense of universality inherited from Graeco-Roman culture and transformed in the light of the faith. It was not an accident that one of the last poets of the Roman Empire, Rutilius Namatianus, already under the influence of expanding Christianity, could write: 'From all the peoples you have formed a single country'.[4] It was no longer the Pantheon, with the gods of the peoples subjected to Rome, which was the sign of peace for the various peoples of the time. What was being constructed now, as the supporting beam and guarantee of peaceful coexistence for the unity of the peoples, was the concept of equality put forward by Christianity. From our first beginnings, in fact, we have articulated and supported with conviction the truth that, independently of culture and of social status, we all belong to one and the same human nature, all have one and the same Father, God, who loves us all without distinction, and that there is one sole Saviour, Jesus Christ. In short, the human city was being constructed on the basis of that which was the city of God.

Of fundamental importance was the joining of the principle of truth to the principle of liberty, a real characteristic of the Christian faith. 'The truth will make you free' (Jn 8: 32) would remain across the centuries the emblem of a originality proper to Christianity, which is without parallel. These foundations and their development in the course of the centuries, which saw the dissolution of the

Roman Empire and the slow passage of the Middle Ages and from there, in the succeeding centuries, the beginnings of modernity, can be open to differing interpretations, but their reality cannot be denied. To repeat this truth is not a matter of making us proud, even though we would have reason to be so, but it is to act as a stimulus to be open to accepting new responsibilities, especially at a time of crisis such as that in which we now live.

Thus, we return to our own times, in which 'crisis' seems to be one of the most used words in our daily vocabulary. We take part in this condition, often helpless or incapable of finding the main road which might lead us out of it. Crisis, however, is never an exclusively negative event; it contains elements which challenge us to express a value judgment about what we are experiencing and it obliges us to find the most suitable ways of moving beyond it. It is possible to think positively also in times of crisis, provided the object of our reflection and the subsequent commitment we make lead us to assess the real contribution the different alternatives before us can make to the bringing about of further progress. From this point of view, we must recall that, at the basis of all civilisation, there are principles which condition and which determine progress, survival or destruction. There are three such principles which are usually acknowledged, *culture, religion* and *law*. It is typical of every society to recognise itself within a *culture* and in those aspects of that culture which distinguish it from other cultures; language, traditions, art in its various forms and everything which constitutes personal and social action and thought form part of what we mean by culture. *Religion,* for its part, is capable of satisfying the fundamental question of human beings as to the meaning of our own lives; that is to say, it provides an answer to the reason for love, pain, suffering, death and to the doubt about whether anything exists after death …, in short, everything which is involved in the question implicit in the claim that the human being is more than what he eats. In human beings there is something which transcends us, an 'infinite' which we ourselves experience in every act of our personal existence and which cannot be suppressed. Finally, there is *law*, that assembly of regulations which regulate social life and which make it possible to identify ourselves within a system of thought and of behaviour which becomes the guarantee for justice, for what is good and what is bad. Precisely this last principle impels us to try to understand how fundamental the relationship between the three elements just described is, such that one does not end up contradicting the other, creating as a matter of fact a short-circuit which would lead to putting a system of life and of thought into crisis.

What is taking place generally in the West, even allowing for the necessary distinctions between different judicial systems, seems to me to be exactly this short-circuit, which impedes a circle of communication between the three principles described, generating as a result the condition of permanent crisis in which we find ourselves. Thus, a situation exists which is paradoxical. In the time, for example, in which Europe lived according to shared principles, it enjoyed a strong identity, which made it easily recognisable as an entity despite territorial boundaries within it. In these recent years, on the other hand, while boundaries have been broken down and so circumstances could favour a process of unification, we find a growth in differences and an increase in forms of extremism; fragmentation seems to dominate to the point where every possible unity seems to crumble. From the perspective of *culture*, it seems to me that certain factors need to be considered. A phenomenological assessment would show immediately the serious difficulties which stem from the fact that Europe lacks a single language, lacks a single form of legislation and lacks the complete adhesion of its different states. There is the impression that, in this process of unification, everything is fixed and determined in advance by an élite, without the direct involvement of the citizens, who are the ones primarily affected. The decision to exclude its Christian roots from the European Constitution was not a good foundation upon which to proceed. Forgetting the traditions in which people recognise themselves may prove to be a mistake because it starts from the presupposition that the new reality to be constructed must be imposed on the basis of a rupture with the past. That is not correct and the mistake made by modernity in having followed that road ought to have served as a warning. We cannot pretend to establish a sense of belonging to a new reality by destroying the identity which people have built up for themselves over the centuries. To think that a single currency could provide an identity or that the exchange of students through the Erasmus Project might create a sense of belonging represents an attitude which is superficial. These are instruments, valid and useful in themselves, but they need to be grounded, accompanied and sustained by a cultural project respectful of differences and yet able to offer the synthesis of something originally new; otherwise everything becomes uniform: language, art, architecture, literature, politics, economy ... In this way citizens become weary, wrapped up in themselves and lose enthusiasm.

If this is what is actually happening, I fear that this depends also upon the fact that people wish to create Europe independently of Christianity and, in some cases, even in opposition to Christianity. Yet, Christianity is a necessary pre-condition for understanding in a coherent manner the history and the present of these countries. The choice of neutrality in the face of religion is the most damaging method it is possible to imagine. The religions of the West cannot all be equal. We are not in a dark night in which everything lacks colour. The primacy of reason, a conquest obtained in the course of the centuries, cannot be reduced right now to an egalitarianism of shifting sands, stifling the voice of our critical powers. The latter is required to discern between religions and to choose to recognise both its own origins and the contribution received from Christianity. Living on the basis of indifferentism, agnosticism and atheism not only will never allow us to come to a response to the fundamental question about the meaning of life, but it will not even allow us to focus upon the objective of the effective unity of the nations.

Therefore, we must not repeat the mistake, already committed, of conceiving of the new reality which is being prepared in terms of a rupture with the past. That is not the way history progresses. It is not by marginalising or exorcising Christianity that we will be able to forge a better society. Such a better society will not be possible. An anti-Christian reading of events is not only short-sighted, but it is mistaken in its basic premises. It will be possible to forge mature identity neither for individuals nor for peoples by leaving aside Christianity. To be sure, our history is made up of a constellation of light and of shadows, but the message we bear is one of genuine liberation for human beings and one of authentic progress for peoples.

Besides, the history of Europe did not begin with the treaties of Rome of 1950. The sharing of resources such as coal and steel, the Euro-atom, the common market, monetary union, are only steps in a process which needs to be able to grasp the underlying sense and the objective to be realised, that is the recovery of the unity of peoples who, even in the diversity of their traditions and of their particular histories, have a common background which goes back to Christianity. Christianity has infused values and formed cultures, creating by strenuous effort but with success a synthesis of Greek and Roman thought re-read in the light of sacred Scripture and a range of successes, cultural, scientific and technological, in the course of the centuries.

In recent decades these values have become oxidised and risk being exposed to a painful wear and tear not due to the passing of the years, but to the corrosion brought about by cultural and legislative phenomena undermining the fabric of society. Having thrown open the doors to presumed individual rights has not led to greater social cohesion and even less to a greater sense of responsibility. What has come about, instead, is a worrying tendency for people to barricade themselves into an individualism which is a dead-end, which sooner or later will suffocate individuals and society. On the other hand, the West seems to be living these days in a profound state of fear. It is becoming almost congenital in populations which, after the barbarities of the two wars, have lived through a long period of reconstruction of increasing well-being and of peace; many certitudes are now wavering because they have been attained, perhaps too quickly and without adequate caution. The stability of the family, education of children, security of work, health services, housing, pensions, ... in short, everything which is generally labelled social progress is creaking under the shadows of a crisis which leaves no room for anything but uncertainty, doubt and anxiety.

How we can emerge from this tunnel, which not only depends on economics and finance, but is primarily cultural and more specifically anthropological, may be easy to see, but it is much more difficult to bring about.

## Beyond the crisis

We do not put forward any legitimate claim of primogeniture to the various achievements brought about in the course of these centuries and which mark the history not only of the West. However, we do not wish that others take possession of them and come to the point of denying our originality and our contribution. If we recall theses facts, and many others could extend the list further, it is simply to repeat that Christianity is not an obstacle to progress in society, but is the condition for genuine social development.

Once again it is the originality of our faith which reminds us how this should be brought about. The lay nature of the state of which we are all so jealous is nothing more than the application of that word of the Lord, 'Give to Caesar what belongs to Caesar and to God what belongs to God' (Mt 22:21). This lay character, as has been increasingly shown during these years, is not the exclusion of Christianity, but a readiness to listen to it to discover what it is able to offer as its particular contribution. To accept or to reject that contribution will be a choice that the legislator will have to assess carefully, not in the light of a handful of votes at the end of the legislature, but on the basis of the good government of public affairs and of the integral cultural formation of future generations. A law creates a resulting culture; this is what ought to be considered in this period of history, in which we can already recognise the consequences of certain provisions enacted into legislation. Is society better off? Have young people found greater commitment and responsibility in society? Has work become a way of realising our potential? Has the family become strengthened within society? Is school the training-ground of life? Is someone who is sick a person to be respected or to be regarded as a burden on the budget? Is life as a whole protected? Is its dignity guaranteed for all? These questions are not rhetorical; it is necessary to give a response to them. If we take as our presupposition what appears today in many areas of our globalised world, namely that primacy is to be given to the freedom of the individual, then it will be a matter of urgent necessity to provide a space for that claim to be counter-balanced by the concrete call to social responsibility.

## *The contribution of Christians*

The first founder of a Christian school in Rome, Justin Martyr, in his *Apologia* directed to the emperor Antoninus Pius, to help him to understand the motivations which inspired Christians, wrote: 'More than all people, we are useful to you and allies of peace'.[5] An echo of these words was provided centuries later by Alexis de Tocqueville:

> The Catholics are faithful to the observances of their religion; they are fervent and zealous in the support and belief of their doctrines. Nevertheless they constitute the most republican and the most democratic class of citizens which exists in the United States; and although this fact may surprise the

observer at first, the causes by which it is occasioned may easily be discovered upon reflection. I think that the Catholic religion has erroneously been looked upon as the natural enemy of democracy. Amongst the various sects of Christians, Catholicism seems to me, on the contrary, to be one of those which are most favourable to the equality of conditions ... On doctrinal points the Catholic faith places all human capacities upon the same level; it subjects the wise and ignorant, the man of genius and the vulgar crowd, to the details of the same creed; it imposes the same observances upon the rich and needy, it inflicts the same austerities upon the strong and the weak, it listens to no compromise with mortal man, but, reducing all the human race to the same stand-ard, it confounds all the distinctions of society at the foot of the same altar, even as they are confounded in the sight of God. If Catholicism predisposes the faithful to obedience, it certainly does not prepare them for inequality ... The priests in America have divided the intellectual world into two parts: in the one they place the doctrines of revealed religion, which command their assent; in the other they leave those truths which they believe to have been freely left open to the researches of political inquiry. Thus the Catholics of the United States are at the same time the most faithful believers and the most zealous citizens.[6]

This echo is amplified in the words of Benedict XVI in his speech in Westminster Hall in London in 2010:

The Catholic tradition maintains that the objective norms governing right action are accessible to reason, prescinding from the content of revelation. According to this understanding, the role of religion in political debate is not so much to supply these norms, as if they could not be known by non-believ-ers—still less to propose concrete political solutions, which would lie altogether outside the competence of religion—but rather to help purify and shed light upon the application of reason to the discovery of

> objective moral principles ... It is a two-way process.
> Without the corrective supplied by religion, though,
> reason too can fall prey to distortions, as when it is
> manipulated by ideology or applied in a partial way
> that fails to take full account of the dignity of the
> human person ... This is why I would suggest that
> the world of reason and the world of faith ... need
> one another and should not be afraid to enter into a
> profound and ongoing dialogue, for the good of our
> civilisation.[7]

Periods of history come and go, as do the persons involved in them; yet, the message remains the same.

The road we are called upon to follow is not easy. The challenges which are placed on our path need to be confronted, analysed and studied in such a way that projects may be created which may correspond to real progress for all. One specific task, however, which is asked of us is to avoid travelling alone. In any event, we cannot do this; we are incapable of it; by nature we are *Catholics*, that is open to all and wishing to be alongside each person to offer them the company of the faith. We want to speak to all, even if we know that not everyone wishes to have dialogue with us. We have all been invited to knock on every door, even though we know that many remain barred. We are convinced that only by means of a deep and reciprocal respect, very much prepared to listen to the reasons advanced by the other, will we be able to travel together fruitfully along a stretch of the road. We do not wish to impose anything, but only to propose; in any case, in terms of the mission which has been entrusted to us, we shall not be found lacking because we believe we can be an instrument of unity between peoples. In this difficult period, however, if some people think they can construct society without us, they will be deluded because the project will not take off. We are the salt which gives flavour, the yeast which brings fermentation; if our contribution were left aside, the dough would not rise and what should stimulate the appetite would remain tasteless.

For this reason we hold that the rediscovery of the identity of the West either will be in continuity with the journey of the last two thousand years or it will be destined to fail. History does not live on the basis of discontinuity, but of continuity, directed towards progress by way of development which unleashes itself dynamically without bringing about any alteration of what put it in motion. On the basis of the experience of history, we are able to affirm that the future is determined by our past and by the capacity of this generation to transmit the patrimony of civilisation and of history to the generations to come. Probably, few civilisations like ours have known an analogous richness of culture and of scientific achievement. If we were simply to repeat the past, we would become quickly boring and incapable of transmitting what generates culture; if, on the other hands, we are able to interpret according to the spirit of our time the patrimony of culture we have received and by which we live, then that richness will grow and with that we shall become significant in writing another page of history.

## Looking to the future

Living by indifferentism, agnosticism and atheism will not help us to bring to realisation a common project because they prevent us from achieving in a full sense the search for the truth. None of us should fall into the trap of thinking about our own country while forgetting that its roots are steeped in a faith which for centuries has fed peaceful coexistence and the progress of different peoples. Thus, there cannot be a modern society worthy of the name which would leave aside our contribution. A sense of belonging to a reality without roots and without soul cannot be imposed on citizens, who differ in their origin and culture; the project will not succeed because the identity requires certainties and these can be consolidated not by means of external instruments, but through the rediscovery of our own common tradition. This creates identity and a desire to belong; otherwise, we will be destined to see prevail the egoism of individuals one after the other and the reaction will be that of enclosing ourselves in new confines, perhaps not territorial, but certainly sources of frustration and of failure. Only a strong shared identity will be able to overcome the fundamentalism and extremism which continually raise their heads in our lands.

In order for this to happen, it is necessary to emerge from the form of neutrality into which many countries have encapsulated themselves in order not to take up a position in favour of their own history. Anti-Catholic episodes, more frequent in these recent years, which have speckled different sectors of society, should promote in the competent institutions an attentive and prompt reaction, at least as strong as that reserved for other religions. If the West is ashamed for what has happened, of the roots which sustain it and of the Christian identity which still forms it, then it will not have a future. The conclusion can only be a that of an irreversible decline. If politics is not capable of a qualitative leap capable of rediscovering a system of values as a point of reference which can overcome the imposition of ideologies, the contribution towards building a common house, which is not limited to the logic of the markets, will be compromised.

Placing once more at the centre of political and cultural commitment some principles of value can only be salutary for the future. In the first place, the *family*, which represents the determining subject of the fabric of society; if we do not wish to do this because of our conviction, then at least let it be done for reasons of economic calculation. The centrality of the family appears to be the trench necessary to prevent the decline of social responsibility which has too often been witnessed already. The primacy of *human life*, from its first instant until natural conclusion, appears to be something of which we urgently need to acquire awareness in the face of the generalised phenomenon of the fall of the birth-rate and of scorn for life, which threatens the survival of civilisation. The slope of ageing populations, along which the West is sliding, reveals the winter season of these countries which have chosen decline, even by imposing a questionable right of the strongest over and above innocent life. To someone in the grip of fear and increasingly isolated, a rapid and mockingly happy death is proposed. The ultimate delusion, euphemistically expressed, is a 'sweet death', as if death did not carry in itself the drama of the ultimate limit of a perennial, existential question, a reality which seeks to be conquered and not endured.

This *slippery slope*,[8] naively embraced by many convinced supporters, is too slippery to be defended as a right; on the contrary, it conceals fear and the overwhelming nature of nothingness because we are unable to make complete sense of our existence. Reference to this completeness becomes all the more urgent the more we become aware of the crisis which we are experiencing. It depends upon a cynical vision of society, tending more and more towards a subtle form of discrimination and even now unable to protect the dignity of the human person. The latter cannot be determined by social status, race, religion and even less by income or physical appearance; it is founded, rather, upon that equality which recognises everyone for who they are and not for what they possess. The fear of the other, frequent enough, basically conceals a fear of oneself, with the refusal of an affirmation of one's personal identity, history and culture. The recognition of a common foundation, which Christianity is, then, is the condition of the success for being able to emerge from an anthropological crisis which is becoming ever more dramatic.

As we may observe, this range of examples stimulates us to reflect upon our capacity to create a process for the transmission of values and contents which form the identity of our peoples, in such a way that these may be rooted, so as to foster the establishment of a significant sense of belonging to a reality which is new, even if it is also old. We Catholics will not stand back from this assumption of responsibility and we

will not accept being marginalised. Our work of new evangelization involves also this dimension. We are convinced, in
fact, that our presence is essential for this process to come to
a successful conclusion. No-one else can take our place in
bringing that contribution which especially belongs to us and
which has marked, in the course of two thousand years, an
unparalleled history of humanisation. Deprived of the meaningful presence of Catholics, our countries would in any case
be much poorer, more isolated and less attractive. We do not
wish this to happen; therefore, we ask that people listen to us
and that they put us to the test to verify once more the richness
of our faith for the genuine progress of society. The hope
which we bear contains something extra-ordinarily great
because it allows us to look at the present, notwithstanding
the difficulties, with a gaze full of confidence and of peacefulness. It is a hope which does not delude because it is strong
with a promise of life which overcomes all limits and fixes our
attention upon the one reality which is truly necessary, a God
who loves and who has shared our human existence.

In short, we have the task of producing a way of thinking
which will lay the foundations for an age which will
provide culture to future generations, allowing them to live
in genuine freedom because they will be orientated towards
the truth. It is this line of thinking which is lacking and, in
all honesty, I do not see it even on the horizon as yet. The
drama, probably, rests entirely in this. If the effort to think
is missing, no-one can claim to have any project to advance
and everything becomes monotonous to the point of
asphyxiation. Who is responsible for devising plans, in
particular for a new anthropology, capable of giving form
to a new model of society? Certainly not one group on its
own. This, then, is the time for a synergy able to provide a
synthesis of the patrimony of the past, to pose questions to
it in the light of the achievements which have characterised
our period of history, in such a way as to transmit them to
the generations which will come after us.

## Notes

1   D. Bonhoeffer, *Letters and Papers from Prison: An Abridged Edition*, (London: SCM Press, 2001), p. 118.

2   It is into this context that the problem rooted in the theme of the end of modernity and of the new 'post-modernity' with its characteristic features must be situated. This is not the place to enter into this argument, already treated in other books. Cf. R. Fisichella, *Nel mondo da credenti* (Milan: 2007); Idem, *Identità dissolta. Il cristianesimo madre lingua d'Europa* (Milan: 2009).

3   G. Lipovetsky, *L'ère du vide* (Paris: 1983), pp. 70–112.

4   Rutilius Namantianus, *De reditu suo*, I, ix.

5   Justin, *Apologia*, XII, 1.

6   A. de Tocqueville, *Democracy in America (1835–1840)*, translated by H. Reeve (The Pennsylvania State University: 2002), pp. 331–332.

7   Benedict XVI, *Speech at Westminster Hall, London, to representatives of British society* (17 September 2010).

8   Translator's note: this expression was in English in the original.

# CHAPTER 4

# JESUS CHRIST AT THE CENTRE

## *The content*

The risk that the ' new evangelization' may appear to be an abstract formula is a real one; to avoid this, it is necessary that it be clarified, so as to highlight those contents which will allow us to grasp its meaning and its purpose. Two expressions seem to me especially helpful for affording greater clarity. The first indicates content and the second points to methodology. The new evangelization draws its strength from the text of the letter to the Hebrews: 'Jesus Christ is the same yesterday, today and always' (Heb 13:8). In him there is no modification or alteration of any kind. What is proclaimed remains identical to that which was there on the first day of our coming to faith. To enter more deeply into the meaning of our verse, we must not forget its immediate context. The author shows himself to have been particularly interested in the cohesion of the Christian community and says: 'Remember your leaders, who announced to you the word of God, consider attentively the nature of their way of life, imitate their faith (v. 7). Unlike numerous texts in the letters of the New Testament, where frequently there recurs the word 'priests' (*presbyteroi*) or 'bishops' (*episkopoi*), here we find the rare occurrence of the word *hegoumenoi*, that is 'leaders', those about whom Jesus, using the same word in the Gospel, says that they must 'serve' while awaiting his coming (Lk 22:26). The context disclosed a little earlier may help our reflection. To the disciples who were discussing who among them was the greatest, Jesus replies that the one who governs must be like one who serves. Addressing this to our own time, this affirmation indicates that, at a time such as that in which we are living, so often confused and tending towards the dominion of power, it is necessary to reaffirm the primacy of true service, which believers are called to discharge. This service must not give rise to pride nor cause us to consider ourselves better than others; it must do no more than make us aware of the responsibility which we must exercise.

The text of the letter to the Hebrews, however, continues, pointing out that the first task carried out by these 'leaders' is that they had proclaimed the word of God. It is precisely preaching which made possible listening and that listening made it possible to come to faith (cf. Rom 10:14), with the support of which the building up of the Christian community could be effected. As we know, proclamation remains the first task of the ministry which Christians are called to discharge; this cannot be abandoned without falling behind with regard to the responsibilities received at baptism. Finally, the sacred author adds something which cannot be considered to be of secondary importance, especially if we think again about our own historical situation; the believer's way of life stimulates others to imitate their faith. The letter to the Hebrews does not allow exceptions; the effectiveness of the ministry cannot be reduced to preaching; rather, preaching must be rendered visible in a witness which offers proof of its credibility. In the union of these various components, from which liturgical action, so important to the teaching of this letter, cannot be excluded, the logic of the faith is structured. To leave aside or to separate these aspects would render vain the very content of evangelization and of the faith. Thus, to believe is not a matter of adhering to a theorem, but is a commitment of life which goes to the extent of self-giving because we have encountered Jesus Christ in a living community which proclaims his name in a way which is credible.

At this point, after having examined the context, the reflection we have undertaken makes possible the next step. This specifies, in fact, what faith received from the apostles and to be preached is, namely the person of Jesus Christ. The expression used by the sacred author is peremptory: 'Jesus Christ is the same yesterday, today and always' (Heb 13:8). There is no room given here for any hesitation and much less for any form of neutrality. In those three adverbs is to be found the solid basis of the revelation of Jesus: he is the 'corner stone' (Mt 21:42), 'the rock' (Mt 7:24–25), the foundation upon which we should build our personal lives. He was such 'yesterday', at the time that is when people came to have faith in him; he is so 'today' when his word is proclaimed and the mystery of his death and resurrection is celebrated, and he will be so 'always' until the end of time. In a word, Christ is always the same. Apart from this, the letter adds something in the following verse: 'Do not let yourselves be led astray by all sorts of strange doctrines; it is better to rely on grace for inner strength' (v.9). It is as if the sacred author had been able to see beyond his own time—certainly something no less easy today—and had fixed his gaze upon the future of believers, when different philosophies and ideologies would attack the stability and the integrity of the faith. There is nothing new in this perspective.

A glance at the letters of the New Testament only confirms this preoccupation. Several times Paul invites his people not to let themselves be cast around by the wind of different doctrines (Eph 4:4), not to subject themselves to regulations and to merely 'human doctrines' (Col 2:22), even putting us on the guard against 'doctrines that come from the devils' (1 Tim 4:1) and those who preach 'another gospel', different from his own (Gal 1:7–9). No less does Peter speak of 'false prophets' (2 Pet 2:1), while John adds to these 'many deceivers' (2 Jn 7). Perhaps the latter is the form today towards which we should be particularly vigilant, the seduction of preachers who, lacking the necessary intellectual preparation, play insistently upon the chords of sentiment, putting forward utopias which, while promising every form of happiness, leave people in even greater loneliness. The chant of the sirens is not the mythology of former times; unfortunately, it is the alluring flattery of our own days. Putting wax into our ears might make things easier and might leave everything in a padded world of illusion. To have the strength of Ulysses and keep ourselves attached to the master tree is not for most people; and yet it is the winning strategy to avoid falling between Scylla and Charybdis.

## Method

The second text to which we refer is the *magna carta* of Christian apologetics: 'Always have your answer ready for people who ask you the reason for the hope that you all have' (1 Pet 3:15). The situation of the early community to which Peter addressed himself is well known; dispersed in different places, fragmented, subjected to numerous difficulties and, not least, the object of various kinds of violence. It was not without reason that the apostle felt the need to remind those Christians:

> You must not think it unaccountable that you should be tested by fire. There is nothing extraordinary in what has happened to you. If you can have some share in the suffering of Christ, be glad because you will enjoy a much greater gladness when his glory is revealed. It is a blessing for you when they insult you for bearing the name of Christ because it means that you have the Spirit of glory, the Spirit of God, resting on you. None of you should ever have to suffer for being a murderer, a thief, a criminal or an informer, but if anyone of you should suffer for being a Christian, then he is not to be ashamed of it; he should thank God that he has been called one (1 Pet 4:12–16).

These words retain their meaning even today in various parts of our small world; notwithstanding such a context, however, believers are called to 'give an explanation (reason)' for the faith.

Apologetics is not extraneous to faith; on the contrary, it belongs with full right to the act by which we enter into the logic of faith. In the first place, it is required that making the act of faith truly be a free act, the fruit of that abandoning of ourselves completely to God by which each one entrusts themselves to him with their intellect and with their will.[1] Giving an explanation of their faith does not seem to have enthralled many believers, at least in recent decades. Perhaps also for this reason, the conviction of faith has declined because the choice was not orientated in that direction. Having recourse to the traditions of old or to all sorts of experiences, but deprived of the power of reason, these have not had the capacity to lead and to sustain, especially when faced with a dominant culture, relying more and more upon the certainties of science. In some respects the situation has become more bogged down, partly because some people have considered that a weary repetition of past forms could constitute a insurmountable bastion of defence, without recognising that those forms were becoming, instead, shifting sands.

To think that the new evangelization can be brought about through a mere renewal of past forms is an illusion not to be cultivated. To be sure, neither is the solution the excess of inventing novelty just to satisfy contemporaries always on the move and ready for any new experience, without even having the trace of a critical approach. The road to be followed is in no sense easy; we need to remain faithful to the fundamentals and, precisely for this reason, to be capable of constructing something coherent with those foundations, but at the same time to be capable of being received and understood by people who are different from those of the past. In any case, in knowing how to 'give an explanation' of the faith and in having to give such an answer, Peter adds three terms, which seem to me to possess a normative value: 'This is to be done with courtesy, respect and a clear conscience' (1 Pet 3:16a). Recalling these three terms has its value for the way we should conduct ourselves. The apostle wants to teach us that the presentation and the proclamation of the hope we carry within us cannot be conducted with the arrogance and pride which come from a certain sense of superiority by comparison with other doctrines. Since the heart of Christianity is Jesus Christ, the encounter with him requires a different approach, one which makes it possible to perceive coherence with the content which is proclaimed.

In the first place he mentions 'courtesy'; this is synonymous with 'meekness' and recalls the beatitude expressed by Jesus. Paul, too, in his letter to Timothy, insists on the fact that 'a servant of the Lord is not to engage in quarrels, but has to be kind to everyone, a good teacher, and patient. He has to be gentle when he corrects people who dispute what he says, never forgetting that God may give them a change of mind so that they may recognise the truth' (2 Tim 2:24–25).

The second element St Peter recalls is 'respect'. This indicates the capacity to understand the person who is asking for an explanation, to be aware that this person has the desire for, and is seeking, what is good; for this reason, it is important to approach everyone, seeking the deepest truth they need, to direct that person by the words we speak towards the truth being sought. To show such respect is also to show a sense of responsibility towards God, because we are announcing his word. That means that no-one may dilute the radical nature of the Gospel nor manipulate it by restricting its contents.

Finally, the 'clear conscience' is equivalent to understanding that, when we proclaim the Gospel, we need to be aware of the coherence of our life, to which we are called as Christians. In short, evangelizers draw strength from the faith and are certain of the hope they carry within themselves, but the way they conduct their lives must be beyond reproach. The justification for this methodology is provided by the apostle himself: 'so that those who slander you when you are living a good life in Christ may be proved wrong in the accusations that they bring' (1 Pet 3:16b).

## Development

As we can see, the path of the new evangelization has been marked out: we are called to renew the proclamation of Jesus Christ, of the mystery of his death and resurrection to stimulate people once more to have faith in him by means of conversion of life. If our eyes were still capable of seeing into the depths of the events which mark the lives of our contemporaries, it would be easy to show how much this message still holds a place of special importance. Therefore, we need to direct our reflection towards the meaning of life and death, and of life beyond death; to such questions, affecting people's existence and determining their personal identity, Jesus Christ cannot be an outsider. If the proclamation of the new evangelization does not find its power in the element of mystery which surrounds life and which relates us to the infinite mystery of the God of Jesus Christ, it will not be capable of the effectiveness required to elicit the response of faith. From this point of view, *Gaudium et spes* indicates a path which deserves to be pursued:

> In fact, only in the mystery of the Word incarnate can the mystery of man find true light ... Christ, who is the new Adam, revealing the mystery of the Father and of his love, reveals man fully to himself and manifests to him his most exalted vocation... Through the Incarnation, the Son of God united himself in a certain sense to every human being. He worked with human hands, thought with human intelligence, acted with a human will and loved with a human heart. Being born of the Virgin Mary, he made himself truly one of us, like us in all things but sin. The innocent lamb, freely shedding his blood, he earned for us eternal life; in him God has recon-

ciled us to himself and with one another and he has
torn us away from slavery to the devil and to sin,
such that each one of us can say, along with the
apostle: the Son of God 'has loved me and sacrificed
himself for me' (Gal 2:20). By suffering for us, he has
not only given us an example that we might follow
in his steps, but he has also opened up for us the way
we are to go; if we follow it, life and death will be
sanctified and will be given new meaning.[2]

In the light of this text which, in some respects delineates a
new anthropology for our age, within the primacy of the
mystery, new horizons are opened up for the pastoral action
of the Church. An initial path is that of the constant search
for the face of God. As Benedict XVI indicated so well in his
speech at the College of the Bernardines, culture is characterised of its very nature by the *quaerere Deum*, the search
for God, and only in this way can it be effective and bring
about progress.[3] That search, strengthened by a tradition
two thousand years long, has been able to enter into
cultures, expressing by means of all the instruments at its
disposal the culminating event of the revelation of God to
humanity. As may be seen, the new evangelization is not
called in the first instance to confront the problem of the
existence of God as a response to atheism. Rather, in the
first place it must renew the presentation of the person of
Jesus Christ and of his awareness of being Son and the one
who reveals definitively the mystery of God. In this context,
within the logic of a process of formation, we must not
forget to present Christianity, in a renewed form, as the
culmination of the phenomenon of religion and, therefore,
as the theme connected with the *true* religion. To leave in
suspension these elements of content for reasons of a
misunderstood form of toleration or to remain passive in
the face of an ever increasing form of control of language
insofar as the expression of Christianity is concerned, would
not be to render a real service to those who have the right
to hear the truth of revelation.

For this reason, it is necessary that the new evangelization find support in a new anthropological reflection within
a framework of apologetics, as the presentation of the Christ
event in a way capable of communicating with our contemporaries. I use this term intentionally because it bears a
positive meaning. 'Apologetics' will lead some readers back
to a pre-Conciliar vision which should be forgotten. Yet,
this would be nothing but a misunderstanding. 'Apologia'
indicates, in the first place, the presentation of the Christ
event as the proclamation of something new which people
were awaiting. To recall in turn the different epochs of
history would be extremely instructive, especially for
checking out the various methodologies adopted.

To be sure, I am aware that precisely a *historical* perspective would require us not to repeat the errors of the past.
For example, I think of the trap into which a form of
apologetics in the modern era fell when it wanted to
respond to certain rationalist tendencies and placed the
whole question at the level of *ratio* and of *demonstrationes*.
It is too dangerous a trap not to understand that, in that
way, *ratio* is elevated to a position of absolute command
and *fides* is reduced to a merely spiritual experience,
relegated to the private sphere and in fact having no
influence. I do not think that we should defend the faith
and thereby the action of the Church first of all on the basis
of external presuppositions and, moreover, fixed by people
outside the Church. The faith has its own power of credibility, which derives from its being in relation, first of all,
to revelation and not primarily to reason. Even when, justly
and necessarily, it is considered in relation to reason, in
order to show its reasonableness, even in this case, it affirms
that the act by which we believe has greater breadth because
it is connected to the action of the liturgy, where the mystery
is evoked and celebrated, and to witness, in which charity
becomes the supreme form of belief. Therefore, it is important that a new apologetic take up the primacy of the
mystery which transforms and converts, and that it be

presented to our contemporaries not in the first place to demonstrate the existence of God or the truthfulness of revelation, but first of all to *show* how, without his presence and closeness to us human beings, we become strangers to ourselves. Love as much as suffering become meaningless and every individual remains isolated in an increasing solitude, in the end with the joy of life wasting away.

## The question of God

Nevertheless, it cannot be denied that the present crisis is connected to the question of God. Therefore, the new evangelization cannot imagine that this question lies beyond its field. To say that it is not the primary question is not the same as relegating it to a place of secondary importance, but rather involves placing it in its proper context. By contrast with the past, today we do not encounter great systems of atheism, if they were ever great; hence, the problem needs to be addressed in a different way. Today God is not denied, but is unknown. In some respects, it could be said that, paradoxically, interest in God and in religion has grown. Nevertheless, what I note is the strong emotive connotation and declining religion in the plural; there is no interest in a religion and much less for the theme of the 'true religion'; what seems to count are, rather, *religious experiences*. People are looking for different modalities of religion, selected by everyone taking up that which they find pleasing in the sense of ensuring for them that religious experience which they find more satisfying on the basis of their interests or needs at the moment. To this must be added that, especially for the younger generations, their horizon of understanding is characterised by a mentality strongly marked by scientific research and by technology. These achievements, unfortunately, already hold the upper hand, even with respect to the basic elements of grammar and to culture in general. Finally, the eclipse of humanistic culture, which is making itself felt in a way which is by now a source of embarrassment and whose consequences are before us for all to see, must not be forgotten. To enter into the merit of these arguments would take us too far from our theme, even though, in many respects, it is strictly connected to them on the basis of the cultural features which stem from them.

To stay closer to the question at hand, it is obvious that it is not correct to enter *tout court* into conflict with science. This must follow its own path and 'God', rightly, is not envisaged as part of it.[4] As Benedict XVI wrote in his encyclical: 'Science can contribute much to the humanisation of the world and of humanity. However, it can also destroy human beings and the world, if it is not orientated by forces which are to be found outside of it … It is not science which redeems human beings. These are redeemed by love.'[5] This fact, though, unless we do not wish to enter into the question of the use of scientific research and the issue of ethics, does no harm to evangelization. The latter does not have as its primary purpose to enter the market of competing theories, but of proclaiming God who reveals himself in Jesus Christ and in him the fullness of the meaning of life is to be found. God affects, first of all, the *personal journey* of all those who are seeking to give a meaning to their own existence, not to indulge in mere academic debate. Hence, God is to be sought beyond science and outside of science, as the requirement of meaning which attains its fulfilment and of personal experience which is lived out. I do not think it pertains to the new evangelization to place itself, in the first place, on the path of the 'proofs of the existence of God', whether traditional or novel. On the other hand, if we wish to take as a model what the Church did at its beginnings, it is easy to point to a different way. Peter's speech on the day of Pentecost, in some ways, becomes normative:

> Jesus the Nazarene was a man commended to you by God by the miracles and portents and signs that God worked through him when he was among you, as you all know. This man, who was put into your

power by the deliberate intention and fore-knowl-
edge of God, you took and had crucified by men
outside the Law. You killed him, but God raised him
to life, freeing him from the pangs of Hades, for it
was impossible for him to be held by its power ...
God raised this man Jesus to life and all of us are
witnesses to that. Now, raised to the heights by
God's right hand, he has received from the Father
the Holy Spirit, who was promised and what you
see and hear is the outpouring of that Spirit...
Hearing this, they were cut to the heart and said to
Peter and the apostles: 'What must we do, brothers?'
'You must repent'. Peter answered, 'and everyone
of you must be baptised in the name of Jesus Christ
for the forgiveness of sins And you will receive the
gift of the Holy Spirit. The promise that was made
is for you and for your children and for all those who
are far away, for all those whom the Lord our God
will call to himself.' He spoke to them for a long
time, using many arguments, and he urged them:
'Save yourselves from this perverse generation'
(Acts 2:22–24, 33, 37–40).

This page in our history is a pointer to a way forward which
is normative, which, in different ways, needs to be undertaken by the Church as a Pentecost which is ever new and
relevant.

Thus, the new evangelization requires the capacity to
know how to give an explanation of our own faith, showing
Jesus Christ, the Son of God, the sole saviour of the human
race. To the extent that we are capable of this, we will be
able to offer our contemporaries the response they are
awaiting. The new evangelization begins once more from
this point, from the conviction that grace acts upon us and
transforms us to the point of bringing about a conversion
of heart, and of the credibility of our witness. Looking to
the future with the certainty of hope is what enables us to
remain rooted neither in a sort of romanticism which only
looks to the past nor to give way to a utopia because we are
bemused by hypotheses which cannot find any confirma-

tion. Faith calls for commitment today while we live; for this reason not to accept it would be a matter of ignorance or fear. However, for us Christians such a reaction is not permitted. Hiding away in our churches might bring us some consolation, but it would render Pentecost vain. It is time to throw open wide the doors and to return to announcing the resurrection of Christ, whose witnesses we are. As the holy bishop Ignatius wrote, 'It is not enough to be called Christians; we must be Christians in fact.'[6] If someone today wants to recognise Christians, he must be able to do so not on the basis of their intentions, but on the basis of their commitment in the faith.

## Notes

[1]   Cf., Second Vatican Council, *Dei Verbum*, n. 5.

[2]   Idem, *Gaudium et spes*, n. 22.

[3]   Benedict XVI, *Discourse to the Collège des Bernardins*, Paris, (12 September, 2008).

[4]   It would be interesting, in this regard, to take up the discourse of St Augustine, with his *comprehendis non est Deus*, which has meaning precisely in reference to science.

[5]   Benedict XVI, *Spe facti salvi sumus*, nn. 25-26.

[6]   Ignatius of Antioch, *Letter to the Magnesians*, 1, 1.

# CHAPTER 5

# THE CONTEXT OF
# THE NEW EVANGELIZATION

## A perennial requirement

Now we must fix our attention upon the commitment to ensure that the new evangelization does not become an all-inclusive formula, including all things and their opposites at one and the same time. This cannot be. The expression 'new evangelization' needs to be understood and explained in a way which is coherent, so that it may be the ground of the Church's activity. Despite all the uncertainties and ambiguities which mark it, it seems the most adequate expression to indicate the requirement which the Church recognises in this particular part of its history, especially in the West.

However, it must not give the impression that at issue is something alternative or parallel to the teaching and action championed by the Church in the twenty centuries of her history. Hence, the 'new evangelization' points to a different modality of fulfilling the same, identical and immutable command of Jesus to his Church, to bring the Gospel to all people. Thus, the content of the new evangelization is not an alternative to the unalterable content of the Gospel; on the contrary, it is the same because it is the proclamation of the name of Jesus Christ, the Son of God, who in the mystery of his death and resurrection has redeemed the world, opening the gate to eternal life to all who believe in him. What is changed, on the other hand, is the mode of expression by means of which the same message is shared, in order to correspond better to the changed social and cultural context. In this particular case, the expression tends to identify Christians who live in cultural contexts in which secularism has created a situation of profound crisis in the faith, with behaviour in clear contradiction to the faith, and who need to rediscover the foundation of their faith. For this reason, the new evangelization is directed first of all to Catholics who live in countries of historic Christian tradition where culture was formed by the faith and who at this time are subjected to being seduced by what is ephemeral, by attitudes of indifference, if not of downright hostility, towards Christianity.

The new evangelization is not something new, introduced by the establishment of a new dicastery of the Holy See. It is something already visible in the daily action of many thousands of people, who in recent decades have taken up this path in order to respond to the invitation of the Blessed John Paul II. There are dioceses, parochial communities, priests, religious orders, new forms of consecrated life, movements old and new, which for years have been living out enthusiastically the experience of the new evangelization and many fruits of their commitment are already visible, especially in the world of the young. The Spirit never ceases to stimulate many Christians, so that, in obedience to him, they may become instruments of conversion. However, in addition to this, the new evangelization is called to identify places where a more innovative pastoral action can be undertaken, a particularly sensitive matter for us today.

## The Liturgy

An altogether special link unites the new evangelization to the liturgy. The latter represents the principal action by which the Church makes manifests to the world its being as the mediation of the revelation of Jesus Christ. From the times of its origins the life of the Church has been characterised by liturgical action. Whatever the community preached, proclaiming the Gospel of salvation, it then made present and alive through liturgical prayer, which became the visible and effective sign of salvation. The latter was not only a proclamation made by eager human beings, but that action which the Holy Spirit effected through the presence of Jesus Christ himself in the midst of the community of believers. Separating these two aspects would be equivalent to not understanding the reality of the Church.

The Church lives by liturgical action as her life-giving lymph for her proclamation and the latter, once it has been completed, returns to the liturgy as to what brings it to its effective completion. The *lex credendi* and the *lex orandi* form one complete whole, within which it becomes difficult in the end to distinguish the end of the one and the beginning of the other. The new evangelization, therefore, will have to be able to make the liturgy its living reality, so that the proclamation which it undertakes may attain its fullest meaning. The plurality of languages and of perspectives in which that proclamation takes place finds an echo in the richness of the liturgy. In fact, the variety of forms of the liturgy and the different rites which make it up show clearly how much the one single mystery can be expressed in different ways without its link to the single apostolic faith ever becoming dissolved.

The daily life within which pastoral activity is discharged allows us to understand even more directly the importance of this relationship and its extraordinary efficacy in a world which more and more needs signs capable of introducing it to the realm of mystery. To make ourselves aware of this, it is enough to think not only of pastoral opportunities, but of the capacity for unveiling meaning which certain celebrations possess. From baptisms to funerals, everyone recognises what a great potential these have within themselves for communicating a message that, otherwise, would not be heard. How many people who are 'indifferent' take part in these celebrations and how many people are often present who are seeking a genuine spirituality! In such circumstances, the word of the priest must be capable of provoking in them the question of the meaning of life, precisely based upon the celebration of the sacrament and of the signs which express it. The liturgy, in fact, is not just a mere rite extraneous to the daily life of human beings, but it is orientated towards its posing of the question of meaning, a question which demands an answer often sought in vain elsewhere. In the celebration of the liturgy, the preaching and the signs are filled with meanings which go beyond the priest and the person of the priest. Here, in fact, the connection with the action of the Holy Spirit allows us to verify the fact that hearts are transformed and that, by his grace, they are formed in such a way as to make them more disposed to welcome that moment of salvation.

The importance of the link between the new evangelization and the liturgy, and between the liturgy and the action of the Holy Spirit, should lead the celebrant to a serious reflection on his ministry, in particular on a matter of great importance, which is that of his homily. Its value for proclamation, for understanding the mystery which is celebrated and for daily life, is so obvious that it leaves no alibi for anyone. To neglect the preparation of the homily or, even worse, to improvise a homily, is a wrong done in the first place to the word of God and, after that, it is a humiliation inflicted upon the faithful. Time dedicated to the preparation of the homily is not time wasted, but it is the condition necessary for exercising the ministry in a way which is faithful, coherent and efficacious.

## *Charity*

One particular field for the new evangelization is certainly that of charity. Entering into this perspective is the equivalent of focusing upon the multiple concrete signs which the Church never tires of presenting to the world. Docile to the action of the Holy Spirit, men and women in the course of two thousand years have identified different places with the intention of rendering visible and present the word of the Lord: 'You have the poor with you always' (Jn 12:8). The present form of 'have' helps us to understand well how the history of the Church can never do without its very special attention to the witness of charity, in which, in fact, is at stake its credibility as to that which constitutes the very heart of its proclamation, namely love.

In his first encyclical, *Deus caritas est*, Benedict XVI illustrated with great clarity the original meaning of Christian love, its source, its development, its special character and the risks of distancing ourselves from it.[1] However, charity is something to be lived out. In the circle which unites faith and love, it is possible to verify the authenticity of the relationship which binds us to the Lord. In fact, in faith we recognise that God is loving; in charity, it is made evident that Christians are faithful to his word. On the other hand, it cannot be forgotten that the way we treat our brothers and sisters is the way we treat God, and vice-versa. Simply giving a passing glance is not possible for the believer. If our eyes are fixed upon Jesus Christ, they must be fixed similarly upon those who hunger and thirst, are strangers, naked, sick or in prison, because in them he is visible. 'Insofar as you did this to one of the least of these brothers of mine, you did it to me' (Mt 25:40) indicates the identification of Christ with the most marginalised and those who are alone, towards whom Christian love is directed. In even more forceful words, the apostle James recalled at the dawning of Christianity:

> My brothers, do not try to combine faith in Jesus Christ, our glorified Lord, with the making of distinctions between classes of people. Now, suppose a man comes into your synagogue, beautifully dressed and with a gold ring on, and at the same time a poor man comes in, in shabby clothes, and you take notice of the well-dressed man and say: 'Come this way to the best seats'; then you tell the

poor man: 'Stand over there' or 'You can sit on the floor by my foot-rest'. Can't you see that you have used two different standards in your mind, and turned yourselves into judges, and corrupt judges at that? Listen, my dear brothers, it was those who are poor according to the world that God chose, to be rich in faith and to be heirs to the kingdom which he promised to those who love him. In spite of this, you have no respect for anybody who is poor. Isn't it always the rich who are against you? Isn't it always their doing when you are dragged before the court? ... Take the case, my brothers, of one who has never done a single good act, but claims that he has faith. Will that faith save him? If one of the brothers or one of the sisters is in need of clothes and has not enough food to live on, and one of you says to them: 'I wish you well; keep yourself warm and eat plenty', without giving them these bare necessities of life, then what good is that? Faith is like that; if good works do not go with it, it is quite dead (Jas 2:1–7, 14–17).

In a period such as ours, often characterised by the individual being closed in upon himself, without any possibility of relating to others and where operating through someone else seems to prevail over any direct form of involvement, this reminder of our responsibility demands a witness which entails that we take upon ourselves this care of our brother who is in greater need. Yet, after all, this is our history. On the basis of the Lord's words, we persist in giving preference to all that the world has rejected, by deeming it useless or inefficient. Persons who are chronically ill, moribund, marginalised, handicapped and much else that, in the eyes of the world, expresses the lack of a future and of hope, these people encounter the commitment of Christians. We have examples which recall forcefully the holiness of men and women who have made of this programme the concrete way of proclaiming the Gospel of Christ and, on the basis of that Gospel, have begun a genuine cultural revolution.

In the face of this holiness, every possible excuse collapses; utopia gives way to credibility and the passion for truth and liberty find a synthesis in the love which is offered without asking anything in return. From this perspective also the witness of *voluntary work* finds its foundation as a genuine form of Christian proclamation. In the different forms in which this is conducted, it becomes ever more obvious that nothing must ever be placed before the dignity of every individual person. In an era in which everything seems to have become possible simply because it can be bought, there ought to be more signs that make it evident that love and solidarity have no other price than personal commitment and sacrifice. This witness shows that personal life finds its fulfilment only when it is referred to the dimension of gratuity. The apostle, Paul, expresses this in very meaningful terms in the letter to the Corinthians: 'What do you have that was not given to you? And, if it was given, how can you boast as though it were not?' (1 Cor 4:7). Love does not live by conquest and possession, but on the basis of gratuity; without this component, everything becomes confused and the risk of not living by love is a real danger. Voluntary work, in the different forms in which it is conducted, calls us back to a primordial experience, that of the gratuitous and sacred nature of the other, wherever they are found and in whatever circumstance they present themselves as neighbour. In the expression of joy or of sorrow, of cultural and social advance, solidarity shows that each one recognises their responsibility, is able to look into things more deeply and to recognise the needs and the true good of the other. Today, various forms of egoism seem to have the upper hand; for this reason, it is necessary to recover those witnesses of solidarity and of generosity who are the more numerous and which are in a position to negate every other contrary form of witness. This commitment to the world, at times marked by contradictions, but one which is loyal, is that which enables us to make the new evangelization a true programme for life and for the transformation of the world.

We cannot be silent, in this context, about the feeling of sadness, which pervades many people who are divorced and remarried, who, in this irregular situation, cannot receive holy communion. This situation, in our contemporary culture, has become ever more common, also among many Christians, and is often the cause of people distancing themselves from the life of the community. It is pointless trying to hide the fact that this is a controversial question; it needs to be explained clearly in terms of the reasons which prevent the Church from responding to the desires of many people who want to come to receive holy communion. The Church too is required to be obedient to the Lord; his command upon her to accept no more than one marriage is binding. It is worth recalling that the state of not being able to come to communion is applicable only to those who, having been divorced, have married again. Divorced spouses who do not proceed to second marriages, either civil marriage or *de facto* unions, do not fall under this discipline and, therefore, as for all other Christians, if the conditions necessary for the reception of communion are there, may receive the sacrament. Attention to Christians who are divorced and remarried should not be neglected, especially in trying to help them see the Church's understanding for them and for the commitment which, even so, they are called upon to live in the life of the community. This requires of them the profession of faith, the proclamation of the Gospel, prayer and witness. I consider that this latter reminder is particularly urgent in the context of the new evangelization.

One point which has always struck me and which could be of paradigmatic significance is this. Everyone knows the greatness of Blaise Pascal, his mathematical genius and his great capacity both for speculation and for spirituality, which find confirmation in his *Pensées*. Perhaps not everyone is aware of one episode in his life. As we know, being a Jansenist, Pascal could not receive holy communion. When he was gravely ill, he asked if he could receive it. It was not possible.

This mathematician and philosopher then insisted on being brought to the hospital of the *Misérables* because, he said, since he could not receive Christ, he might at least be able to share the fate of the poorest of the people. This he was not allowed to do; he was a noble and could not be found in a place like that. Then he asked insistently to have a poor person next to his bed; in fact, only in this way, not being able to receive Christ in holy communion, could he see Christ present close to him in the person of the pauper. Not even in this was his request granted. However, at the end of his life, he was able to receive holy communion and to die in peace with the Church.

This impressive fact may help us to understand what kind of commitment may be expected of someone who cannot receive holy communion; it is the witness of charity. If you cannot receive Christ, you can keep yourself in his service in the poor, among whom he is present. How many opportunities are offered even today in the face of old and, unfortunately also new, forms of poverty! I am afraid that, in some cases, continuing always and only to focus on not being able to receive communion can become a justification for not committing oneself, soul and body, to the service of charity. On the other hand, in his letter, the apostle, Peter, writes explicitly: 'Love covers over many a sin' (1 Pet 4:8). To look at the face of Christ, reflected in that of the person in need and to relieve his suffering and poverty, is an act of charity which shines in the sight of God, especially if it is undertaken in a way which is hidden and silent.

## Ecumenism

We refer now to the commitment in culture, about which we have spoken in the preceding pages, by reason of the massive presence of a secularism which is expanding the deserts in which our contemporaries find themselves. In a context as important as this, we cannot imagine that the commitment to the new evangelization can be conducted unilaterally. The Second Vatican Council has allowed us to consider relations with other Christians of other Churches and confessions in a way which is new, compared to the past. The West has to take account of the presence of Christians unfortunately divided among themselves, but the challenges posed by culture are identical for all. However, it cannot just be this challenge which stems from such difficulties and from a common crisis which impels us to seek a shared commitment. At the origin of evangelization is the command of the Lord, directed to all baptised persons, to go into the whole world to communicate the mystery of his love. The renewed commitment embraced in the new evangelization, therefore, can be a project which we share and conduct with a common effort and cause on the part of all Christians.

In think particularly of the serious problems existing in society in those countries which have experienced Marxist and communist dictatorship. There the spiritual desert is an undeniable reality. Reading the pages written by the patriarch of Moscow, Cyril, *Freedom and Responsibility seeking Harmony*, like those of Hilarion, metropolitan of Volokolamsk, in his book, *Christian Witness for Uniting Europe, The point of View of the Russian Orthodox Church*, both confirm the same perspective. Besides, many evangelical communities live in the same situations of crisis which disturb us as Catholics. Sunday attendances present worrying statistics and the sense of belonging to the community is more and more fluid.

In many countries in the West, amongst other things, esteem and fraternity between the various communities can make possible collaboration because one and the same Gospel of Jesus Christ is known by all. To be sure, for the credibility of our proclamation, division among Christians is not a factor of secondary importance; rather it gives rise to questions, provokes unease and weakens the proclamation itself. The words the Lord left us identify in the sign of unity not only the fact that we belong to him, but above all they give witness to the fact that he was sent by the Father: 'I pray not only for these, but for those also who through their words will believe in me. May they all be one, Father; may they be one in us as you are in me and I am in you, so that the world may believe it was you who sent me' (Jn 17:20–21). It is essential, as we follow the indications of the Holy Spirit along the pathways of the new evangelization, that we not close ourselves off from his action to convert our hearts. We urgently need to overcome the divisions of the past to live out responsibly the mission of being the visible and concrete sign of the unity of all the baptised.

## Immigration

One last object of reflection is the phenomenon of immigration. The West is living today in a situation very different from that of the past, in respect of which it is not important for us to examine its social consequences, but its impact in regard to the new evangelization. It would be good to consider at least three aspects. The first must recognise that in the past the phenomenon had already been encountered. In many countries the influx of immigrants stimulated the various Churches originally there to take care of those immigrants. This happened in the nineteenth and twentieth centuries, with great examples such as St Francesca Cabrini and blessed Scalabrini. However, up to our days, a country such as Italy has known the great generosity of many priests who left their homes to follow Italian immigrants into various European countries and who even today fulfil their mission in the light of a new evangelization. The same experience is presenting itself again in our time, as various churches send their priests into our countries to provide spiritual assistance for an increasing population of immigrants.

A second element is the immigration in recent decades with millions of Christians arriving. Europe, the United

States, Canada and Australia are well aware of the presence
of immigrants from Eastern Europe, Latin America and the
Philippines, the majority of whom are Catholic. These are
a source of richness, not only economically, but also for the
new evangelization. Contemporary society is often pitiless
and tends to swallow up in a whirl of indifference these
new immigrants, preventing them from preserving their
faith and their traditions. This is an attitude which should
be challenged. Our communities ought to be open and
welcoming because their tradition, still a living reality, can
represent a richness capable of challenging our indifference.
To be sure, the popular piety which is part of the immigrants' experience requires there to be a sharing of a deeper
knowledge of the contents of the faith. Still, the new
evangelization lives also on the basis of this fruitful
exchange of traditions, which express respect and comple-
mentarity.

A third aspect is constituted by the presence of mass
migrations of people of other religions. These express the
desire of human beings for relationship with the Absolute
and manifest ancient traditions of wisdom. The seriousness
and the uprightness of heart with which they seek God is
a road which can lead to encounter with Jesus Christ and
often this is what happens. Citing the words of St Eusebius
of Caesarea, the Council, in the dogmatic constitution on
the Church, *Lumen gentium*, affirms that these religions can
be 'a preparation for the Gospel'.[2] The new evangelization,
like evangelization in general, cannot exempt itself from
the explicit proclamation of Jesus Christ to all people, so as
not to impede someone from being able to come into contact
with the saving word. With the respect which is due to all
and with the prudence required by different situations, the
new evangelizers cannot proceed without meeting also
those who do not believe the Christian faith. If the proclamation may not be received at times, that does not mean
that we cannot find a sharing of values in the promotion of
life and of its dignity and of that of creation.

## Communication

A final field for our attention is furnished by the complex world of communications. In the apostolic letter founding the Pontifical Council, the task is explicitly entrusted to it by the Pope of 'studying and fostering the use of the modern forms of communication, as instruments of the new evangelization'.[3] A glance at what is happening at the present demonstrates that the instruments of communication are no longer pure instruments, but that they constitute an authentic expression of culture. The new evangelization is taking place in the also in the midst of this new *mediapolis*. Various voices, from sociologists and psychologists, make themselves heard to put us on guard against dangers underlying this new 'little big world' of the Internet, which is spreading and which presents problematic traits, especially as to its influence on personal and on mass behaviour.

However, the world of communications cannot be considered only in its functional aspect; that would be a dangerous mistake. It would not only distance us from this world of communications, but it would prevent us from understanding it in its real nature and under the different forms of which it is composed. To think of the world of communications in terms of pure technology is reductive and does not help us to see the real face of the culture which it embodies. In actual fact, we are faced with a universe of thought and of technologies with enormous potential, at present perhaps only partially known and used.

For good and for bad, from wherever we look at this media world, it appears more and more like a modern market place from which the Christian cannot remain estranged. The language which is being built up through the new form of communication, therefore, deserves to be known, studied and, insofar as this is possible, used, without betraying the message which we bear, in view of fostering a clear and effective understanding of that message. In some respects, finally, we need to confront this new world because already it determines our culture, together with the language and the behaviour which stem from it.

Communications experts, however, will not be able to under-value the strong communicative power that Christianity possesses. With reference to the new evangelization, we must be in a position to make the signs, for example of the liturgy, intelligible. In the first place, I think of the evocative language proper to the liturgy, which enables us to grasp its meaning only by referring us to the mystery which is perceived and which our words cannot completely make explicit. The capacity to express the value of prayer and of liturgical gestures in images and in the appropriate setting is a form of communication that would be extremely useful to the new evangelization. In particular, I refer to the value of silence. In a society such as ours, strongly characterised by noise and loudness, transforming itself at times into a bombardment of notices, the cine-camera could just run images and accompany them by silence, so as to allow each individual the opportunity to offer their own mind the chance to learn the profound value of reality. What communicative power there is in signs and what a great need we have of professionals in this field who are also believers! On the one hand, priests ought to be capable of a communication which is respectful and coherent with the mystery, without having recourse to abuses which often cause offence because of their typically clerical arbitrariness. On the other hand, communications experts ought to help us with their professionalism to make the perception of the sacred and of the mystery real.

**Notes**

1    Benedict XVI, *Deus caritas est*, 2005.
2    Second Vatican Council, *Lumen gentium*, n. 16.
3    Benedict XVI, *Ubicumque et semper*, art. 3 n. 4.

# CHAPTER 6

# PROSPECTS

## A recent challenge

Some of you were perhaps surprised to see the title of this Congress *Evangelization 1947* ... Does this not perhaps fall into the common obsession of wanting to renew everything, at least at the level of words? Must evangelization also be subjected to these changes? Is the Gospel then no longer the same as before? Certainly not! Evangelization always aims at the same purpose, it aims at spreading the same truth, a truth which has not changed and which will never change. But what has been capable of change, what necessarily has had to change is the manner in which the message is spread. For entire centuries the Church has found herself faced with a world which is Christian. I am convinced that, also in what once upon a time were called the Christian centuries, there were serious defects and at times sad betrayals, but I know too that then those who had been guilty had a precise awareness of their responsibility for that wrong; they were accused of these things as of something immoral and they sought in their faith, which had remained alive, the secret by which they might pick themselves up again. Nowadays, instead, we find ourselves faced by a world which is pagan, which rejects *en bloc* all the duties of the Christian, which does not seek a faith and which is capable only of remorse, and which at times quite wilfully seeks to present as progress or as a liberation infidelities brought about to the damage of the Christian

tradition. In the face of such a transformation—and
who would dare to deny that such exists?—you
must understand that the methods cannot remain
what they were. You say to me: 'But are you not
exaggerating?' Look around. Has the world suffered
or not from a deep de-Christianisation? It could also
be said, not unjustly, that for many human beings,
we cannot properly speak any longer of de-Christianisation because it is a question of people who have
never been Christian. The causes of this de-Christianisation are numerous.[1]

This text comes from a speech of Cardinal Pierre-Marie
Gerlier at the end of a congress on the theme of evangelization in 1947. Since then much water has flowed under the
bridge; still the words of the cardinal of Lyons retain all
their force, both in terms of their provocative form and in
terms of the questions, which are the same now as they were
then. Probably, the evidence of de-Christianisation today
is such that these words may even appear to be obvious,
given the territory concerned, whose limits extend already
far beyond the Alps and the Pyrenees.

## The cultural scene

We live in a time of great challenges, which coincide not a
little with the patterns of behaviour of entire generations
and which are to be attributed to the conclusion of one
epoch and the entering into a new phase in human history.
To the many positive elements brought about by the
progress of science and technology and by the ever more
conscious commitment of so many persons in the field of
faith, it is not unusual to find opposed to these both forms
of discrimination and of social marginalisation which were
unknown to our experience until a few generations ago and
also expressions of a distancing from faith, the consequence
of a diffuse form of religious indifferentism, the prelude to
practical atheism. Very often the lack of knowledge of the
basic contents of faith and of culture lead people to assume

behaviours and forms of moral judgment in contrast with those principles on the basis of which civilisation was erected in the course of twenty-five centuries of history. The relativism, whose limits and who contradictions Pope Benedict has always condemned, precisely in view of a coherent anthropology, emerges as the distinctive characteristic of these decades, marked ever more by the consequences of a secularism which tends to drive our contemporaries further away from their fundamental relationship with God. In this sense, it is especially in Churches of ancient Christian tradition such as ours which experience this sense of contradiction: the human being is alienated ever more from himself and is exposed to an interior desert without precedents in the centuries which have gone before.

It is thus urgent that we construct a project, whose object will be to restore to Christians a strong identity as believers in terms of the contents of the faith which sustains them and one which is rich in terms of a deep sense of belonging to the Church, capable of recovering its value of community. In the two thousand years of Christianity what has been constantly verified is that the Christian community has been permanently attentive to the times in which it lived and to the culture within which it was inserted.

A reading of the apologists, of the Fathers of the Church and of the various doctors and saints who have succeeded one another in the course of these two thousand years would show very easily this attention to the world around and the desire to become involved in it, to understand it and to orientate it towards the truth of the Gospel. This attention was grounded upon the conviction that no form of evangelization would have been effective if the word of God had not entered the life of persons, into their way of thinking and into their activity, to call them to conversion. To proclaim the Gospel effectively necessarily requires, in the first place, familiarity with the word of God, which allows those who listen to it to verify in themselves not only the knowledge of the Gospel, but above all its credibility, which is expressed in a way of life coherent with it.

A first consideration, therefore, must never be lacking when we speak of new evangelization, that is to say the profound *cultural change* which we are experiencing. We must understand that, in the face of a pathology, we need to find the appropriate medicine; otherwise everything will be in vain. The pathology which is afflicting our world today is of a cultural character; it is essential, therefore, to come to know it and that we find the right remedy to overcome it and, if this does not happen, pastoral initiatives will be multiplied, but they will be ineffective because they will be incapable of reaching their objective. Anyone who is immersed in culture as a child of their time, can extract themselves from it only with difficulty to understand the phenomena which lie at the base of its way of thinking and of acting. To adapt oneself to such a movement, unfortunately, becomes an almost 'natural' fact, for which reason behaving differently would be equivalent to finding oneself marginalised from the social context. It is important, therefore, to seek to delineate the *cultural* space into which the new evangelization is inserted, without relegating the latter to a secondary role, because that would be to jeopardise the efficacy of the proclamation and of the initiatives in its regard which it is intended to put forward. We cannot allow ourselves to live with the illusion that our language of faith can be understood and accepted to the same extent as it always was and by repeating the same things from time to time, because this is not so.

## *The mission of the Church*

However, I would like to make clear a principle of fundamental importance. The Church does not evangelize because she is placed before the great challenge of secularisation, but because she must be obedient to the Lord's command to bring his Gospel to all creatures. In this simple thought we find condensed a project for the coming decades which obliges us to understand fully the responsibility which lies upon the Church of Christ in this particular period of history. The Church exists in order that, in every age, she may bring the Gospel to every person, wherever that persons is. Jesus' command is so crystal clear as to admit neither of misunderstandings nor of alibis. All who believe in his word are sent out along the roads of the world to proclaim that the salvation promised has now become a reality. This proclamation has to be united with a style of life which allows people to recognise the Lord's disciples wherever they may find themselves. In some respects, as I have said a number of times, evangelization is summed up in a style of life which marks out those who give themselves to following Christ.

We could spend a long time discussing the meaning of the expression 'new evangelization'. To ask whether the adjective determines the noun is a reasonable question, but it does not affect the reality The fact that it is called 'new' does not mean to qualify its contents, but the way in which it is conducted. In the letter *Ubicumque et semper*, Benedict XVI rightly underlines the fact that he considers it appropriate 'to offer responses which are adequate, so that the whole Church may present itself to the contemporary world with a missionary dimension, capable of promoting a new evangelization'.[2]

It might be insinuated that to decide to undertake a *new* evangelization is equivalent to judging the pastoral action previously conducted in the Church as a failure on the basis of its negligent application or because its members lacked credibility. Even such a consideration is not without all plausibility, apart from the fact that it limits itself to a phenomenon of a sociological order, looked at from a partial perspective, without taking into account that the Church in the present world is also marked by constant holiness and by credible witness, which still in our days are marked by the sacrifice of people's lives. The martyrdom of many Christians is not different in fact from that offered in the course of the centuries of our history, even if it is truly *new* because it provokes people of our time, often indifferent, to reflect on the meaning of life and on the gift of faith.

When the search for the genuine meaning of life is lost and we move along paths which lead us into a wood of ephemeral proposals, without us realising the danger awaiting us, then it is right to speak of a *new* evangelization. This appears as a real stimulus to take life seriously, to give an orientation towards a meaning which is complete and definitive, which finds its confirmation in the person of Jesus of Nazareth. He, the Revealer of the Father and his historical revelation is the Gospel which we proclaim even today as the response to the question which has always bothered human beings. To put ourselves at the service of human beings to understand the anxiety which propels them and to propose a way out which will give them peace and joy is what we gather from the good news which the Church proclaims.

Therefore, a new evangelization is needed because the context in which our contemporaries live is new, as often they are buffeted about here and there by out-dated theories and ideologies, However paradoxical it may seem, people often prefer to impose their own opinions on others rather than to direct themselves to the search for the truth. The need for a new language capable of being understood by the people of our time is a requirement from which we may not prescind, especially in regard to religious language, so much marked by technical details that it is often no longer comprehensible. To open up the 'language den', to foster a communication which is both more effective and fruitful, is thus a concrete commitment so that evangelization may be really 'new'.

## Truth and love

One theme which the new evangelization will inevitably have to address touches upon the great question of *truth*. The *quaestio de veritate* is not a treatise from other times nor an archaeological discovery to be confined to museums for the sake of a *politically correct* race which imposes the obligation to avoid all clarity, whether theological or doctrinal, and to lower everything to the superficiality of the commonplace or of widely held majority opinions. The truth continues to present itself as a *quaestio*, which asks to be submitted to the test of reason, to bring yet another rich element of wisdom into personal and social life.

An initial question to which an answer is needed, in any event, may be formulated like this: is it really necessary in our time to speak of truth? In fact, we are experiencing a time of poverty, of unease, of lack of confidence in the ability to attain truth; to first to pay the price for this is religion. Very rarely is faith presented as radical newness of life which calls for conversion, but we remain fixed on the fact of an anonymous Christianity which all can understand without ever being disturbed by it; in the end, we prefer to remain silent about differences, leave conflicts in the shadows, to smooth down the edges. In short, we are afraid to measure up fully to the question of truth. If evangelizers lose the passion for truth, then the proclamation will fall into rhetoric and, unfortunately, will become meaningless. It is necessary to put forward once more and with *parresi* (boldness) the value of veracity, that is of love for the truth. This has a face, that of Jesus of Nazareth. The Johannine expression, which brings out the revelatory awareness of Jesus, 'I am the way, the truth and the life' (Jn 14: 6), remains as the originary fountain of our understanding of truth.

A renewed presentation of the issue of 'truth' is accompanied by some themes strictly connected to it. First of all, the vision of *gift* which is offered. In such a sense, it is interesting to check out the great propelling power which a theme like that can have in the context of pastoral work, especially in terms of verifying the relationship between truth and love. In a time like ours, in which love seems to be subjected to a spectacular contradiction, it is not super-

fluous to try to recover its relationship with truth to
establish the wealth and the fecundity with which it con-
tributes to pastoral action on a daily basis, in particular that
directed to the world of youth. That love hides within itself
the essence of personal life is one of the truths which appear
among the most evident.

It is a complex matter to try to explain how people of our
time have been able to effect such great harm to their
existence, reducing love to passion and confounding it with
a poorly concealed form of egoism. In the same way it is
sad to confirm, that in some cases, there has been a slide
towards an attitude which can be considered to be one of
mere philanthropy, which qualifies our structures as service
agencies without any great motivation, rather than being
witnesses to gratuitous love. Nothing more than love needs
to be brought back to its basic truth and, in a reciprocal way,
nothing more than truth needs to be made visible in love.
As there exists a faith which seeks reasons for its own
existence, so love must be able to look for an understanding
of itself. Paul's expression 'truth in love' (Eph 4:15) shows
the essence of the relationship. In some respects Benedict
XVI's encyclical closes the circle by affirming love in truth
(*caritas in veritate*). Love finds its form in truth and it cannot
be otherwise.

The Church has a deep responsibility towards the world,
in particular on this theme. Not only do we need to grow
in knowledge of Christ, but we need to so in such a way
that believers may be able to develop the style of life which
follows as a consequence. Our pastoral action must foster
a growth on the way to salvation which make progress, step
by step, with our maturity as individuals, who are rooted
ever more deeply in the truth of faith. The apostle recalls:
'then we shall not be children any longer or tossed one way
and another and carried along by every wind of doctrine,
at the mercy of all the tricks men play and their cleverness
in practising deceit' (Eph 4:14). It is as if to say: error and

deceit do not allow us to have a stable life and, much less, are they capable of stimulating personal growth.

Hence, truth is not only in relationship with love, but it stands within love and expresses itself through love. In this way, truth *in* love implies that it is love which decides the way in which truth is to be expressed. Accustomed as we are to parcelling out truth and, paradoxical as it seems, having become theoretical defenders of each fragment, here, in this way, we find ourselves faced with the possibility of tending towards the totality of truth on the basis of its permanent basis in love. This is not a sentimental love which is illusory, but a love which has as its purpose the welcoming of the truth of the other insofar as we recognise in that truth the same foundation from which our own truth proceeds. A truth in love, then, is the real challenge which is launched at this period of epochal change. It has the characteristics of a sharing and a welcoming, such that these values become promoters of that true progress which, in the Church and in society, we all need.

## The Sacrament of Confession

In a very popular television transmission of quiz games, one of the challengers was asked to what the 'sacrament of reconciliation' referred. They had to choose between four possibilities which were offered. Not knowing how to answer, the challenger asked the help of the public, which, in its secret vote, gave the wrong answer in 75% of the cases. As a theologian I should speak of the sacrament of reconciliation, but to be understood by the reader, after the television transmission, I prefer to speak of confession, the synonym more widely diffused in common language and more easily understandable.

This theme is not outside of the contents of the new evangelization. On the contrary, it enters into it with full rights because in this sacrament there can a real experience of what was noted previously: the love and the truth of our own existence. It is a matter of urgency that pastoral care place the sacrament of confession and spiritual direction, if not at the centre of its activities, then at least in their proper position. In reconciliation, in fact, it is possible to rediscovery a confluence of themes of great relevance to the change we are undergoing. I think, first of all, of the loss of the sense of sin, which derives in part from the loss of the sense of belonging to the community. If we do not have a community of reference, it is very difficult to understand and to judge our own style of life. Locked each one into their own individualism, our contemporaries are no longer capable of this comparison and they give way to the illusion that each one's style of life depends on them alone, without there being any need for social responsibility.

The sacrament of confession obliges the person to accept the value of truth in their own lives because it establishes a link with a community which, for good or ill, considers the person to be part of it. Life, made up of ideals and of contradictions, needs forgiveness as an experience of love and of mercy. Confession makes it possible to attain both aspects, allowing the penitent himself to become an instrument of pardon A society like our own, which seems to have forgotten pardon and which fosters an increasing number of reactions of violence, rancour and vendetta, needs witnesses to pardon and signs of mercy.

However, if we do not experience directly the condition of being loved and for this reason forgiven, it becomes difficult to think of how such signs can be provided. Confession is the efficacious instrument which transforms human beings. Nor must we forget, finally, the need to place ourselves before the truth of our own lives, without any illusions. In a period in which the sense of omnipotence pervades many and in which we confound dream and reality, thinking that everything can be obtained or is our exclusive personal possession, returning to take account of what we are in reality would not be a cause of harm to us, but, rather, it is an urgent necessity.

# Identity and belonging

A further reflection is called for. The new evangelization tends to make our sense of personal identity grow in relation to our sense of belonging to the community. A sociological tendency of our time presses us to distinguish between 'identity' and ;belonging', as if it were a question of two contradictory realities. The first would be subject to a form of conservatism, on the basis of its recalling our own traditions and paradigmatic models; the second, on the other hand, would be the emblem of progress, insofar as it tends to underline the plurality of segments which, together, discover forms of living together in society within which we can recognise ourselves.

There is nothing more dangerous, in our opinion, than this contra-position. A belonging which was without identity could not be defined as belonging; it would remain always bound to a form of living together in society which modified its own coordinates according to the changing of the seasons, without any possibility of impressing upon them a real sense of common feeling and of active participation.

To understand more completely the value of belonging, it might be useful to recall its semantic meaning in the German language. In German, in fact, 'belonging' is called *Zugehörigkeit*,[3] which of itself indicates the capacity for listening.[4] The consequence is immediate. Belonging equates in the first place to listening, but listening is connected to a *tradition* which transmits the conquest of a patrimony of wisdom in culture. Tradition is a permanent language which is kept alive precisely by the sense of belonging of the members who transmit a content. Belonging, in short, indicates a process of transmission which is strengthened by knowing how to listen by looking in a far-sighted way at the new demands hidden in the world. Hence, it is in this way that new forms of belonging can be created which do not alter, but which develop identity, keeping their own roots alive.

From the reciprocal relationship which exists between identity and belonging, therefore, there arises the possibility of verifying how the new evangelization can be effective and fruitful. Without a strong Catholic identity, by means of which our awareness of our own responsibilities in the world may grow, it will not be possible to understand even the requirement of belonging to the Christian community; on the other hand, without a deep sense of belonging to the Church, it will not be possible to have an identity which is aware of the mission it discharges.

Identity and belonging determine our understanding of the permanent formation which applies to Christians in view of an ever more adequate knowledge of the faith, one which corresponds to each one's own state of life. A knowledge of the contents of the faith which remains linked to the adolescent stage could never allow someone to grow in their identity as a believer, no matter what roles they might occupy in civil society. In the same way, the lack of these contents often impedes people's own social, political and cultural action in harmony with their belonging to the Church. A fissure between identity and belonging is prob-ably one of the causes which has contributed to the current crisis.

## Catechesis

To confront a subject such as formation requires that we introduce some considerations on catechesis in connection with the new evangelization. Even a rapid glance at the history of the Church shows that one of the principal activities of the bishop was catechesis. St Augustine's *De catechizandis rudibus* is only one of the examples from our rich history. The deacon Deogratias at Carthage was charged with the responsibility of catechising catechumens and writes to the bishop to ask his advice as to how to conduct himself. The difficulties which the deacon confided in St Augustine, in some respects, could be considered identical to those of our days. The holy bishop replied to the discouraged deacon that catechesis has to be anchored in the history of salvation such as the word of God reveals it to be, but the catechist must be capable of adapting the language and the teaching to every culture and to every person to whom he addresses himself, in such a way that all people in all places may be offered the possibility of believing. How much this advice remains valid today can be shown from the fact that we are so far removed from new forms of language as often to render our preaching vain.

John Paul II recalls that 'in relation to the new generations a valuable contribution, more necessary than ever, must be offered by lay faithful by means of a systematic work of catechesis'.[5] This is a decisive chapter in the life of the Church because it tends towards the promotion of a Christian conscience ever more aware of the role it has to play in the community and in society. Certainly, one of the more serious problems of the present portion of history is the profound ignorance of the fundamental contents of the faith. The situation becomes even more dramatic the more we observe the learning of scientific culture, which is not going ahead at the same rate as that of the faith. In some respects, rather, the latter is being relegated to the mere experience of youngsters and adolescents; thereby the conviction is created that catechesis is a matter for them alone, but that it has nothing to do then with adults. Christian formation is a necessity for growing in the faith and no-one may consider themselves exempted from this. Therefore, catechesis constitutes one of the elements of such a formation and it is essential to the work of the new evangelization. In fact, by means of catechesis we attain a systematic knowledge of the mysteries of the faith and we understand much better the value of witness. Hence, in such a context, it is as urgent as the work of new evangelization itself. Called to give an explanation of the faith, the Church will never be able to accustom herself to having only a very small group of believers capable of providing such an explanation.

Responding to a request of the bishops gathered in 1985 to celebrate the twenty-fifth anniversary of the closing of the Second Vatican Council, John Paul II published the *Catechism of the Catholic Church*. In the apostolic constitution, *Fidei depositum*, he wrote as follows: 'this Catechism will make a very important contribution to the work of renewing the entire life of the Church as wished by the Second Vatican Council ... I recognise it as a valid and legitimate instrument in the service of the ecclesial community and as a sure norm for the teaching of the faith'.[6] As has been noted, the *Catechism of the Catholic Church* is an important instrument because it gathers within itself the whole patrimony of growth in the understanding of the faith over two thousand years. The Sacred Scriptures, the Fathers of the Church, the Masters of theology and of spirituality, the examples of the saints ... all are brought to a harmonious and systematic synthesis to make the reason for believing understandable. Not only that. It represents also an unusual effort of intelligence and of collaboration, to the point that it constitutes the 'fruit of a collaboration of the whole episcopate of the Catholic Church'.[7]

The importance of the *Catechism of the Catholic Church*, however, lies in its being an instrument necessary for the new evangelization, insofar as its makes it possible to demonstrate the unity which inter-relates the act by which we believe and the contents of the faith. A tendency which is very widespread in our times, but one which is extremely dangerous, attempts to justify our being Christians independently of our knowledge of those contents of faith. In fact, the act of belief is justified precisely by the knowledge of the mystery to which we give our own assent; on the basis of this knowledge, a knowledge at once global and unitary, belief is a free act of the person rather than a weary gesture of belonging to traditions. Finally, the *Catechism of the Catholic Church* can assist the new evangelization to overcome a difficulty which is present in different churches, which limit catechesis to the sacraments alone, an approach which in our time has exposed its own limits. If it is directed to the sacraments, it seems obvious that, once the preparation for the sacraments of initiation has been completed, there is the risk of falling away in relation to further formation. It is time to take up once more and with conviction a process of continuing formation, directed to all believers, while showing respect for the different stages and methodologies, but whose objective is the understanding of the Christian mystery in view of a way of life which is coherent with what we believe, a perspective which, once again, finds in the *Catechism of the Catholic Church* a valuable instrument. Indeed, its very structure reveals the extent to which the Christian life must develop on the basis of the profession of faith (part I), to liturgical celebration (part II), from the moral life (part III) to prayer (part IV). This is constant progression, which shows both the unity of the mystery of faith and the demand for a Christian way of life in conformity with it.

## A new anthropology

One theme of great importance which we are called to face is the question of anthropology. Having underlined in the preceding pages that the present crisis is concentrated in a different vision of the human being requires us to deal with attempts to emerge from the crisis in a way which consistent with that claim. For this we shall require an effort of great intensity, so that Christians may be able to offer their contribution to the establishment of a new anthropology. John Paul II recalled this in words which were far-sighted when he wrote in his first encyclical, an encyclical which was the programme of the pontificate, *Redemptor hominis*:

> Jesus Christ is the principal way of the Church. He himself is our way 'to the Father's house' and he is also the way to every human being. On this road, which leads from Christ to the human being, on this

road on which Christ unites himself to everyone, the Church cannot be blocked by anyone. This is the essence of the temporal good and of the spiritual good of us all. In order to look at Christ and by reason of that mystery which constitutes the life of the Church herself, the Church cannot remain insensitive to anything that serves the true good of human beings, just as she cannot remain indifferent before what threatens it ... The Church cannot abandon the human person whose 'destiny', that is whose choice, calling, birth and death, salvation or perdition, are so closely and indissolubly united to Christ. And this is a question of every human being on this planet, on this earth ... Every human being, in his or her irreplaceable reality of being and of action, of intellect and of will, of conscience and of heart. The human being, in his or her unique reality (because they are 'person') has their own history of their life and, especially, their own history of their soul. The human being who, in conformity with the interior opening up of his or her spirit and together with so many different needs of their body, of their temporal existence, writes this personal history by means of numerous connections, contacts. situations, social structures, in which they are united to other men and women and what they do from the first moment of their existence, on the basis of their being which is both personal and at the same time communitarian and social – in the setting of their family, in the setting of society and of its many different contexts, in the setting of their own nation or people (or perhaps still only of their clan or tribe), in the setting of humanity as a whole – this human being is the road which the Church must take to fulfil her mission; the human being is *the first and most fundamental way of the Church*, the way traced by Christ himself .[8]

From this perspective it seems necessary to overcome the nihilistic vision of reality, in order to set a perspective of meaning which makes its own the theme of the human being as the image of God, a person open to relationship, created out of love and destined for love. In its work of new evangelization, the Church cannot withdraw herself from this challenge. Perhaps the effort will seem titanic, beyond the forces available, and utopian. Perhaps. Nevertheless, if the Christian is not convinced in the certitude of his or her faith that 'nothing is impossible for God', then they would have to pull the oars back into the boat and live resigned to their situation; 'resignation' in this sense, however, is not a concept known to Christians. Belief confers upon us the courage to know that, even with faith the size of a grain of mustard seed, we can say to the mountain: 'Move' and it will do so (cf. Mt 17:20). A difficult project could frighten us, but without any project at all, we would be to be pitied.

What I personally see ahead of us is the requirement to finalise a model of humanism capable of bringing about the necessary synthesis between the fruit of what has been achieved in the preceding centuries and the more scientific and technological sensitivities on the basis of which we interpret our present. In some respects, I would like to spot on the horizon a *new humanism*, a term to which I refer intentionally because it bears a weight of meaning justly acquired over the course of centuries. It represented a fundamental stage of development for culture. In fact, in its time, humanism unleashed a genuine enthusiasm which affected all areas of human activity; its good fortune was precisely the freshness of the movement which embodied the spirit of the times, which managed to reinterpret in a new way the problems there had always been. Humanism was the capacity to understand the changes which were taking place, but it expressed also the conviction of being able to re-read, and in some respects to resolve, the problems that had always troubled humanity. It did not have a fragmentary vision of the world, but a unitary vision, also in the sense that its analysis placed the human being at the centre of creation. In this phase, which extended from philosophy to literature, from art to the discovery of new lands, God was not excluded, but became the horizon of meaning for personal research and for social life. A humanism in which the passion for truth acquired in the past became the real impulse of transmission for a culture which was strong and with great creative incisiveness, because it was a sign of the achievement of knowledge, for whose safeguarding and reinterpretation everyone felt responsible.

To re-create this humanism is the task which stands before all of us and its realisation cannot be achieved in a way which is unilateral. We Catholics wish to make our particular contribution, no differently from in the past. In our heart we have the destiny of peoples and of individuals because our history has made us 'experts in humanity'. The Gospel, which we transmit from one generation to the next, is the proclamation of a new way of living, brought about so that we may overcome our supreme fear, death as annihilation of self. People should not be afraid of the Church, those who presume to know it only by means of an indirect reading of what she is, one which is from a distance and often the product of erroneous pre-conceptions. To be sure, in the course of our history, some people have made mistakes and we all feel some responsibility for this. But the Church cannot be identified with the action of individuals. She goes beyond the bounds established by conventional agreements and does not stop at the fragmentary action of individuals; the Church is the continuation of the risen Christ and is his effective presence in the history of every age to be the instrument of unity for the whole human race'.[9]

Some might be afraid or fearful that our action intends to destroy the achievements of modernity, to which they are particularly attached. Nothing could be further from the truth. In us there is no desire to destroy those achievements which are true, brought about in the course of the centuries; we could not do that, we would not be capable of it and we could not contradict centuries of history. If today the world recognises the richness of the patrimony, philosophical, literary, artistic and juridical, of the ancient *athenea* of Rome, they owe it to us Christians. Animated by our conception of living tradition, we were established to preserve what the wisdom of human beings has brought about and not to destroy it; if anything, we feel responsible for purifying it of accretions, which the inevitable contradictions of humanity bring with them. Besides, no-one can deny that the great achievements established over time find their basis in Christianity. The concept of the lay nature of the state, of freedom of equality, the fundamental rights of the person ..., none of this would have had a fruitful outcome if it had not found endorsement in the concepts of person, of dignity, of seeking the common good, which are the cornerstones of our social vision.

The centrality of the subject, upon which the modern world is constructed, does not upset us; on the contrary, it stimulates us in every age to identify new categories which may help us to understand that a coherent anthropology can be constructed only if openness to the transcendent, capable in itself of welcoming God, the stable foundation for true freedom, is recognised. Analogically, the concept of forgiveness as the expression of a love that is capable of going beyond offence, is that which has moulded entire generations of peoples and has made it possible to build up a more profound brotherhood and solidarity.

The concept of matrimony which Christianity introduced as the uniqueness of relationship in the reciprocity of love has guaranteed justice in the face of the arbitrariness which humiliated defenceless women and the power of the inter-personal relationship as the binding force of the social structure. The search for the common good, with respect for the dignity of every person, does this not derive as such from the concept of person which Christianity has produced as its contribution to the patrimony of humanity, from the fourth century onwards? Respect for life, especially for innocent, weak and defenceless life, is a further sign of the presence of Christianity in the social structure which has made it possible to generate extra-ordinary intuitions in the work of assistance, of solidarity and of subsidiarity which, unchanged, even now are sure points of reference for society.

Furthermore, it is necessary to recall that the defence of reason finds in us allies who are loyal and faithful; we could never think of a faith which was strong before reason which was weak. We are supporters of a reason which is strong, capable of sustaining a faith which is free, precisely because it is the fruit of a reasoned choice in the face of truth. The foundation of a correct approach to the relationship between reason and faith is to be ascribed to our thinking, which has never wished to humiliate reason, but which has made of it an indispensable companion on the road. It is hard, in the context of a phenomenology of world religions, to discover a relationship as well-balanced between these two components as in Christianity.

For our tradition the *fides quaerens intellectum* is the condition necessary for us to reach every man and woman, in every part of the world. For us rationality is a common criterion which sustains the fundamental equality between persons. It is on the basis of the positive relationship with reason that conflicts can be avoided and that every form of fundamentalism from which the world suffers can be excluded. The latter is the expression of a fragment of truth which is then rendered absolute without taking into consideration any longer the contribution of others, who are excluded on the pretext of the supremacy of one's own truth. For us, this is not so. For us, truth is given by way of revelation, but it has entered into history with the incarnation of the Son of God and this makes it inevitably subject to the law of its constant and dynamic path of interpretation and activation until the end of time.

Moreover, it is precisely the concept of the salvific value of the truth which has allowed Christians to make it a universal achievement and not a good subject to variations of price according to the needs of the market. John Paul II recalled this in a particularly forceful way when he wrote in *Fides et ratio*:

> This today appears even more clearly, if we think of that contribution of Christianity which consists in the affirmation of the universal right to access to the truth. Having broken down racial, social and sexual barriers, Christianity had proclaimed from its very beginnings the equality of all people before God. The first consequence of this concept was applied to the theme of truth. The characteristic, held by the ancient thinkers, that the search for the truth was a matter for an élite was decisively overcome; since access to the truth is a good which allows us to reach God, all people must be in a position to be able to travel along this road. The ways to attain the truth remain many; nevertheless, since Christian truth has a salvific value, each of these paths can be pursued, provided it leads to the final goal, in other words to the revelation of Jesus Christ.[10]

## Notes

1   P. M. Gerlier, *Discorso di chiusura*, in AA.VV. *L'evangelizzazione* (Roma: 1950), pp. 229-230.

2   Benedict XVI, *Ubicumque et semper*, preamble.

3   Translator's note: *hören* = 'to hear' or 'to listen'; *zuhören* = 'to listen to' or 'to belong to'.

4   See H. G. Gadamer, *Truth and Method* (London: Seabury, 1975).

5   John Paul II, *Christifideles laici*, n. 34.

6   Idem, *Fidei depositum*, n. 1.4.

7   *Ibid.*, n. 1.

8   Idem, *Redemptor hominis*, nn. 13-14.

9   Second Vatican Council, *Lumen gentium*, n. 1.

10  John Paul II, *Fides et ratio*, n. 38.

# Chapter 7

# New Evangelizers

## *Our common calling*

We cannot conduct a new evangelization without new evangelizers. This is not a tautology, but it is a fact which, however, cannot be taken for granted. We find written in the letter of St Paul to the Romans:

> All who call on the name of the Lord will be saved. But they will not ask his help unless they believe in him, and they will not believe in him unless they have heard of him, and they will not hear of him unless they get a preacher, and they will never have a preacher unless one is sent, but, as Scripture says, 'The footsteps of those who bring good news is a welcome sound' (Rom 10:13–15).

As is known, the first idea that the letter communicates is that of the relationship between the need to invoke the Lord, to have faith in him, and being sent to proclaim him so that all may believe. At the foundation of this mission is to be found the calling; this stems from the invocation to mission because it recognises that Jesus Christ is the Lord of each and of all. Therefore, to be an evangelizer is to have a vocation, so that all may hear the Gospel of Jesus, believe in him and invoke his name. This vocation is born on the day of our baptism and calls on every believer in Christ to make himself a credible bearer of the good news which is embedded in his teaching. To be invited, therefore, is intrinsic to the baptismal vocation; this implies that every Christian assume the responsibility in his or her own person, without any possibility of delegating this to anyone else. The proclamation of the Gospel, in fact, cannot be delegated; rather it demands an awareness on the part of every believer of making himself or herself a bearer of Christ wherever they may go. We have witness to this conviction even in the most ancient writings; Saint Cyril, the bishop of Jerusalem, spoke in his catecheses in this way: 'Having received in ourselves his body and his blood, we are changed into being bearers of Christ'.[1] Thus, the Christian, by his very nature, is *Christophoros* and only in this way can he manage to understand the meaning carried by the Lord's words: 'Shoulder my yoke and learn from me, for I am gentle and humble of heart, and you will find rest for your souls. Yes, for my yoke is easy and my burden light' (Mt. 11:29-30).

## One sole Priesthood

We cannot forget that there exist different ministries within the Church. These, though founded on the common mission to proclaim and to give witness, are lived and are exercised in a different way according to the vocation proper to each one of us. The first evangelizer is certainly the bishop. Insofar as he is a successor of the apostles, upon him is conferred the mandate of being in the world a loving icon of a proclamation which is courageous and strong. He cannot remain silent; his experience of the Risen Lord obliges him to give witness. Peter's expression, the day after the Easter: 'We cannot be silent' (Acts 4:20), notwithstanding the restrictions imposed by the leaders of the people and the threats of violence, must permeate our lives as a pastoral imperative from which we cannot remove ourselves. The difficulties which arise from such a silence are not always appreciated; the words of the bishop of Hippo, Saint Augustine may come to our help:

> From the time this weight was placed upon my shoulders, for which I will have to give an account to God which will be far from easy, I have always been tormented by the worries of my dignity. The most dreadful thing in the exercise of this responsibility is the danger of preferring my own honour to

the salvation of others. However, if on the one hand I am afraid on account of what I am for you, on the other I am consoled by the fact that I am with you. For you, in fact, I am a bishop; with you I am a Christian. The former is the name of a charge I have received, the latter is a name I have received by grace. The former is a source of danger, the latter of salvation. In truth, we find ourselves in an immense sea, battered by storms, precisely because of the pastoral charge which has been entrusted to us. We remember, though, at the price of whose blood we have been redeemed and, consoled by this thought, we enter as if into a safe harbour. While we labour at apostolic work, the certainty of the common benefit which derives from it comforts us. 'What shall I give to the Lord for all he has done for me?' If I say that I offer to the Lord the ministry of pasturing his flock, I speak the truth. I do this, in fact 'not I, but the grace of God which is in me' And so, my brothers, 'We exhort you not to receive the grace of God in vain' Make our ministry fruitful. 'You are the field of God' (1 Cor 3:9). From outside you receive those who plant and who water, from within, on the other hand, you receive him who gives the growth. Help us with your prayer and your obedience, that we may find our joy not so much in being your leaders so much as in being servants of use to you.[2]

Therefore, no bishop may forget that at the moment of his consecration he promised and declared before the whole Church that he would 'preach faithfully and perseveringly the Gospel of Christ ..., guard pure and entire the deposit of faith, according to the Tradition preserved always and everywhere in the Church from the times of the apostles.'

The mission of evangelising, proper to the bishop, is shared with priests who participate in it and who, along with him, form the *one single presbyterate*, that is a single priestly body placed at the service of the People of God to proclaim and to keep ever alive his word, in a way which is united to the celebration of the action of the liturgy. In his homily proclaimed in Cyprus in June, 2010, Benedict XVI made use of an interesting expression in this regard: 'The Church has gained a renewed awareness of the need for priests who are good, holy and well prepared. She desires men who submit themselves completely to Christ, dedicated to spreading the kingdom of God on earth. Our Lord promised those who offer their life in service and imitation of him that they will keep it for eternal life' (cf. Jn 12:25).

Three expressions are particularly relevant for our theme. The Church needs, the Holy Father said, priests who are good, holy and well prepared'; he added 'who submit themselves completely to Christ' and 'who are dedicated to spreading the kingdom of God'. These are the elements which are necessary, in which in some way there is con-densed a theology of the priesthood for our time, in view of the new evangelization. A careful analysis of these words would allow us to construct the identity of the priest for the contemporary world in his mission of bringing the Gospel always and everywhere and notwithstanding anything. Amongst other things, it is necessary that we establish the challenges which are present in the priestly life, in order to be able to evaluate their impact and to find the way of addressing them.

However, when we speak of pastoral challenges, we are tempted to consider whatever the world places before us as an obstacle. This is true only in part. The first challenges which we need to understand and to which we must give a response come directly from within the Church and from our being priests. To the extent that we are capable of accepting and of making our own these challenges, we shall be in a position to recognise in their true dimensions those challenges which the world presents and which today's culture makes ever more evident, as an expression of the great changes which require our contribution and response.

The first challenge, therefore, is that which leads us to verify the meaning of being priests in the world of today, to understand fully the significance of the vocation. In fact, the priesthood is neither a human achievement nor an individual right, as many today seem to think, but it is a *gift* that God brings about for those whom he has decided to 'call' to 'remain with him' in the 'service of the Church'. To lose sight of this vocational dimension would be equivalent to misunderstanding everything and to making the priest an employee and not a man who fulfils a ministry under the sign of complete gratuity. To share this first perspective allows us to relate the priest, in the first place, to the reality which makes sense of his condition, the Eucharist. The real challenge consists precisely in understanding ourselves in relation to the mystery which is celebrated and which makes of every priest a minister of Christ. The Eucharist remains as a gift which can never be extinguished which has been made to the Church and to every priest personally; for this, respect and devotion are due, without ever claiming to operate as masters of the mystery of which, instead, we are servants. In his ministry the priest must not put his person, with his opinions, to the fore-front, but Jesus Christ. If, in the liturgical action, a special element of his ministry, the priest becomes the leading character, this would contradict his very identity and would render vain the ministry itself. The priest is 'servant' and his work is effective to the extent that it leads to Christ and he is perceived as a docile instrument in his hands, to collaborate with him in the work of salvation.

To live on the basis of the Eucharistic mystery leads us to accept another challenge, which impels us to confront the individualism, spirit of the contemporary world, with that of the *communion* which priests are called to live as brothers who form a single community. To form one single presbyterate around the bishop means also to live with a love which is true and real, which, following the Master's example, is lived out in a full and total complete gift of self to all, without asking anything in return. It means to leave everything to live together with the Lord in a celibate love which knows how to recognise all those who are in need and in solitude, to go to meet all. This communion which priests are called to live calls us back once more to the preceding theme; in the first instance, it is communion with the 'Body of Christ'. *Life*, to use the term pregnant with meaning of the evangelist John (1 Jn 1:2), has become visible and is now placed in our hands in the sign of the Eucharistic bread. To sum it up, priests become capable of acts which exceed their personal existence in itself because they act *in persona Christi capitis*, in the person of Christ the Head. In other words, the conviction must be strong in every priest of being 'clothed in Christ' and for this reason capable of a new style of life, which makes evident to all that we are living for an Other to the point of making him visible in our own lives.

Fixing his gaze upon the Eucharist, for the priest, is the equivalent of finding the foundation of the whole of his existence, what enables him to make sense of his ministry and what gives him certainty in his vocation. Feeding himself on the body and blood of Christ means for him the bringing about of a unity so indissoluble, 'in one body' with the Lord, that he may not participate in any other sacred meal nor share his body with others. 'Anyone who is joined to the Lord is one spirit with him ... Now you together are Christ's body, but each of you is a different part of it' (1 Cor 6:17, 12:27). Paul could not find a stronger expression than this to express the basic unity which lies at the basis of Christian existence and, *a fortiori*, of the priestly ministry. To be dispossessed of oneself to become the body of Christ is the witness provided by the sacrament of the Eucharist. St Augustine expresses this equally forcefully when he writes: 'If you, then, are the body of Christ and if you are his members, on the table of the Lord is placed your sacred mystery; you receive your sacred mystery.'[3] This is to say that, on the Eucharistic table, the meaning of the priestly life is celebrated.

The mystery that the priestly vocation represents becomes understandable if it is inserted into the greater mystery of Christ the Eucharist, which makes it possible for us to verify the extent to which a calling may be a sign of a service which lasts all through life in forgetting self in order to give oneself to the brethren in his name. As if they were an echo extending throughout history, the words of the holy bishop of Antioch, Ignatius, come to mind: 'Be sure to maintain one Eucharist. One alone is the flesh of our Lord, Jesus Christ and one alone is the chalice in the unity of his blood. One alone is the altar as one alone is the bishop, in union with the priests and the deacons, my fellow servants. If you do this, you will be doing the will of God.'[4]

Another of Benedict XVI's texts may introduce the next point: 'This audacity of God who entrusts himself to human beings; who, even though he knows our weaknesses, considers us capable of acting and of being present in place of him, this audacity of God is the truly great reality which is hidden in the word "priesthood". That God considers us capable of this, that he calls men to his service in such a way and so, from within, binds them to himself.'[5]

These words make it possible for us to understand better the condition of the priest in the contemporary world. He is the sign of the audacity of God, who considers that a man, with all his fragility, is capable of rising to the point of being an icon of his own presence in human history. His audacity is linked to the confidence he places in the priest; the latter, even with all his contradictions, is capable of transforming the lives of persons. If we reflect seriously on this reality, it is possible to confirm what great anthropological value is hidden in the person of the priest and in his vocation. In fact, this represents a real challenge for the construction of a new anthropology, capable of responding to the great question that today lies on the table, how to unite the truth about ourselves with the freedom of a choice which makes it possible for us to fulfil ourselves.

It is undeniable that one of the features of the culture which today we have to face is that of freedom. The latter poses itself as one of the constitutive principles of modern thought and it is placed at the foundation of rights which many invoke as inalienable on the basis of their own dignity. A freedom which was separated from truth, however, would have only a short life and would easily fall into the temptation of being expressed as the power of the strongest and most arrogant over the weakest and those without any voice.

To speak to our contemporaries about the freedom with which we dedicate our life to the Lord in the service of the Church requires reference to truth as the horizon of meaning to bring about the fulfilment of our personal identity. This is why a new anthropology is urgent, within which the choice of the priesthood can also be placed as an expression of genuine freedom, precisely because it its united to the truth. It is a question, in the end, of establishing a principle according to which a person is truly himself or herself at the moment when they answer the plan of salvation which God wants for the each one of us. The completion of our own life, which makes it possible to see brought to harmonious fulfilment both truth and freedom, is brought about in the daily discovery of a plan which is not bounded by the limits of individual existence, but which projects us beyond ourselves into a personal relationship with God who entrusts himself to a concrete individual, entrusting to him a task as great as it is impossible to fulfil without a divine calling.

We can understand at this point the value of the word 'audacity' to express God's courage in wanting to choose a priest to keep his Gospel alive and make it possible for human beings to have a true and effective relationship with him. In fact, audacity shows that God is not afraid to entrust such a decisive mission to a man. Rather, he is aware that he is running a great risk in thinking of his person; still, he does not draw back. Into every priest he infuses the courage to face a task which is extra-ordinary, to transform the life of persons in their intimate depths.

It is enough to think of some of the signs the priest discharges to understand the greatness of his position. At the moment he extends his hands over the head of the penitent who confesses his sins, not only does he absolve in the name of God, but he transforms his existence to such a point as to re-admit him to the life of relationship with the Father and in communion with the community. The same thing happens when he extends his hands over the bread and the wine and pronounces the same words Jesus used at the Last Supper: in a real way every priest transforms that bread and that wine into the body and blood of Christ. This does not happen through others; it can occur only if a priest extends his hands and pronounces those words. He has the power to change the world. Yes; because the lives of persons are transformed, these are rendered capable of living wherever they find themselves as living witness of the Gospel of Christ and this is a real action of transforming society and the world.

Therefore, the priest is in a position to accompany the people of his time, to give them the certainty of the presence and of the closeness of God. And he becomes the sign of this presence, so that no-one may be deceived when he turns to God. How can we gain access to God and be sure we are praying to him? In what way can we enter into relationship with him, if he is transcendent and is the thrice holy? Is a life of love of him truly possible? These questions are not new, they belong to humanity from the beginning; on the other hand, the objections of Freud and of Marx, even though in different terms, are repeated in our time when people speak of faith and of prayer as a 'useless hypothesis', 'fruit of a psychosis', a 'path of alienation'.

The most convincing response to these questions comes from the letter to the Hebrews. The sacred author claims that, to draw close to God, we must offer a worship that is *truthful* and that this is not possible without the intervention of a priest who is worthy of that name. What makes him worthy? First of all, he must be 'pleasing to God' and 'admitted into his presence'; besides this, he must live in solidarity with those whom he represents before God. The letter, however, recalls that 'no-one attributes this honour to himself; it happens only if we are called by God ' (Heb. 5: 4).

The themes of vocation and of gratuity remain highly relevant, with all their power and depth of meaning. Following the example of Christ the 'high priest', every priest after him too is called to be pulled between belonging to God and solidarity towards human beings. Both aspects need to be amalgamated together in such a way as never to be separated. If the life of a priest were only in reference to God, it could not communicate with human beings; by contrast, if the gaze of the priest were fixed only on solidarity with people, he would not be able to communicate God to them.

In a period such as ours, often torn by various conflicts of a social, political, economic and financial order, which generate delusion, suffering and confusion, it is not surprising that the priest finds himself tempted to choose between one road or the other. That would be fatal for his mission of evangelization. In these times, in fact, it is possible to open up the road to search for spirituality and for God. The priest, therefore, must not be unprepared to respond to the demand for a more intense search for God and for the spiritual life. All of this will be possible to the extent that he is faithful to his ministry.

The value of audacity returns once more, with all the force of its meaning. An example of this occurs in the *Diary of a Country Priest* by Bernanos.[6] Re-reading this not only fosters a serious examination of conscience, but heartens the soul, knowing that the conclusion he reaches is the fulfilment of the priestly life, 'Everything is grace'.

It is interesting to observe that the country parish priest does not have a name. As the novel proceeds, we learn bit by bit the names of all those affected by his pastoral action, the people who come to him and the priests he meets, the parishes nearby and the country round about; in short, we know everything except the name of the priest. He does not possess a name of his own because his is the face of every priest, identical in every place throughout the world. There is no intention to eliminate his personality; on the contrary. His character is described very well, his way of thinking and of behaving, in his daily reflections, in the joy of a ride on his motor-cycle and in the spasms of permanent pain which will lead him to his death …, he is not an unknown. Not giving him a name, nevertheless, is the equivalent of having exalted to the level of an icon the way of life of a priest. He is truly audacious. He is the sign of someone who brings hope to a woman who for years lived in sadness and in anger against God on account of the death of her child of a few years of age; even in the midst of the difficulty of such a conversation, he opens her heart to welcome the love of God who has given his entire self in the gift of Jesus on the cross.

All of this was possible because the parish priest of Ambricourt finds in Jesus his companion along the road, through the streets of his parish and his friend in moments of extreme solitude. In fact, it is to Christ that he speaks in his *Diary*; he is his true confidant and he is the only one capable of entering into the folds of his life, to comfort him at every step. On the other hand, there emerges clearly in his eyes, especially when faced with situations of indifference, of atheism and of the abandonment of the priesthood, that he himself had chosen to make of his life an *imitation of Christ*. If the priest were capable of penetrating into the depths of the mystery of which he has direct experience, he would understand with greater awareness the audacity of God. This would become for him a further source of encouragement to place his entire self at his service, proclaiming that *fiat* which is the most coherent form of obedience, disposed to allow himself to be transformed by grace.

## Consecrated persons

A service of fundamental importance for the new evangelization is provided by consecrated persons. First of all, these people are called by their vocation to live a style of life which calls them in the first place to the holiness towards which the whole Church is directed. This style of life is expressed visibly in the evangelical counsels lived out in community; by means of these counsels, such people aim to manifest the novelty and the radical nature of following the Lord. While, on the one hand, poverty, chastity and obedience express fully the act of the free choice of consecration, on the other hand, they make evident the way of the Gospel as the form of life which deserves to be followed and to be lived out. This consecration becomes an instrument of the new evangelization. This John Paul II recalled with great clarity in the apostolic exhortation *Vita consecrata*:

> The common life plays a fundamental role in the spiritual way of life of consecrated persons, both in terms of their constant renewal and in terms of the full realisation of their mission in the world ..., following the example of the first Christians in Jerusalem, who were assiduous in listening to the teaching of the apostles, in common prayer and in sharing the goods of nature and of grace (cf. Acts 2:42–47). I exhort especially religious men and women and members of societies of apostolic life to live without reserve the life of reciprocal love, expressing this in ways which are consonant with the nature of each institute, so that every community show itself to be a luminous sign of the new Jerusalem, 'the dwelling place of God among men' (Apoc 21:3). The whole Church, in fact, counts greatly upon the witness of communities 'rich in joy and in the Holy Spirit' (Acts 13:52). She wishes to point out to

the world the example of communities in which mutual attentiveness helps people to overcome solitude, communication leads everyone to recognise a sense of co-responsibility, forgiveness brings those wounded back into the fold, strengthening in each one the purpose of living in communion. In communities of this kind, the nature of the charism directs people's energies, sustains them in their fidelity and orientates the apostolic work of all towards the one common mission. To present to human beings of today its true face, the Church has an urgent need of fraternal communities like these, which, through their very existence, constitute a contribution to the new evangelization, because they make manifest in a concrete way the fruits of the 'new commandment'.[7]

We cannot forget that in the history of past centuries many religious orders arose precisely with the purpose of evangelization. For many consecrated persons, the path of their mission has been the vocation to follow and it has been very fruitful in the life of the Church. Millions of men and women, young and less young, have left their families and their countries to become missionaries to peoples who had not yet known the name of Jesus. In the same way, faced with the urgency of the moment, many have become 'new evangelizers', making of the mission to the nations the instrument for a renewal of the life of faith.

In recent decades the Holy Spirit has also inspired new expressions of the consecrated life, to respond to the changed needs of the times. It is not a question of alternative models to those of the past, but of expressions which correspond better to the world of today, which asks for further signs of holiness. In the one case as in the other, the words of John Paul II remain relevant:

Adequately to face up to the great challenges which the present phase of history poses to the new evangelization, in the first place a consecrated life is needed which allows itself continually to be

addressed by the revealed Word and by the signs of
the times. The memory of the great female and male
evangelizers, who were the first great evangelized,
demonstrates that, to face the world of today, we
need persons loving, devoted to the Lord and to his
Gospel ... The new evangelization, like the evangelization there has always been, will be effective if it
knows how to proclaim from the housetops everything its proponents have first lived out in intimacy
with the Lord. For this, we need people with solid
personalities, animated by the fervour of the saints.
The new evangelization demands of consecrated
men and women *full awareness of the theological
meaning of the challenges of our time.* These challenges
must be examined with careful and joint discernment, in view of a renewal of mission. The courage
of the proclamation of the Lord Jesus must be
accompanied by the confidence in the action of
Providence, which is at work in the world and which
'disposes everything, even human adversity, for the
greater benefit of the Church'. Important elements
of a fruitful insertion of the institutes into the new
evangelization are fidelity to the charism of foundation, communion with those in the Church who are
involved in the same task, especially with pastors,
and cooperation with all people of good will. This
demands a serious discernment of the calls which
the Spirit directs to each institute, whether in those
regions where great progress is not foreseen in the
immediate future or in other regions where a com-
forting rebirth has been announced. In every place
and situation may consecrated persons be ardent
messengers of the Lord Jesus, ready to respond with
evangelical wisdom to the questions posed today by
the worries of the human heart and by its most
urgent necessities.[8]

## Lay people

A very special role is played by lay people. Under this term
we gather together the whole complex and differentiated

reality of the Church, of the baptised called to live the experience of faith in parishes, in associations, in movements and that incredible galaxy afforded by the action of the Spirit which is constantly at work for the mission of the Church of Christ and which does not admit of any boundaries to its activities. In the light of the specific teaching of the Second Vatican Council on the laity, the bishops returned anew to this subject to describe their vocation and the mission entrusted to them in the life of the Church. The document *Christifideles laici* (1988) constitutes a real patrimony of theology and of spirituality to understand the irreplaceable role which lay men and women hold in this particular moment of history.

The Council's constitution on the Church, *Lumen gentium*, contains an interpretative key which is completely original and decisive for understanding the contribution of the laity to the new evangelization. We read: 'The laity are called above all to make the Church present and operative in those places and circumstances in which she cannot become salt of the earth unless by means of them'[9] It is exactly the phrase 'unless by means of them' which ought to stimulate our reflection on the special contribution which lay people are called to bring about. In other words, it is obvious that there are circumstances and contexts which can be reached by no-one, if not by lay men and women who are able to give witness to the faith by means of their professional life. Their presence in these settings is irreplaceable and only they are in a position to bring that first form of humanisation which is often the necessary prelude to speaking about Jesus Christ.

The synodal document seems to offer an explanation in regard to this. Introducing the theme of the new evangelization in relation to the action of the laity, it says:

> Whole countries and nations where the Christian religion and life were once thriving and able to give rise to communities of living and active faith are now very much put to the test and at times have even

been radically changed by the continual spread of indifferentism, of secularism and of atheism. It is especially a question of countries and nations of the so-called First World, in which economic well-being and consumerism, even if mixed with frightful situations of poverty and misery, give rise to and support a life lived 'as if God did not exist'. Now, religious indifferentism and the total practical insignificance of God for the even major problems of life are no less worrying and subversive than that of declared atheism. The Christian faith too, even if it survives in some of its traditional and ritualistic manifestations, seems to be uprooted from the more significant moments of existence, such as the times of birth, suffering and death. From this situation formidable questions and enigmas emerge, which, left without answer, expose contemporary human beings to delusion without any source of comfort or to the temptation to eliminate human life itself which poses those problems.

In other regions and nations, on the other hand, living traditions of piety and of popular Christian religiosity have been preserved up to the present, but this moral and spiritual patrimony risks being lost through the impact of many processes, among which are secularisation and the spread of sects. Only a new evangelization can assure the growth of a faith both clear and deep, capable of making of these traditions a source of strength of authentic freedom. Certainly it urges us to rebuild everywhere the Christian fabric of human society. But the condition is *that the Christian fabric of the ecclesial communities themselves*, living in these countries and nations, *be rebuilt*. Now, the lay faithful, by reason of their participation in the prophetic office of Christ, are fully involved in this task of the Church. In particular, it is for them to give witness how the Christian faith constitutes the only fully adequate response, more or less consciously perceived and invoked by everyone, to the problems and the hopes that life poses to every human being and to every society.

> This will be possible if the lay faithful will be able to
> overcome in themselves the division between the
> Gospel and life, reuniting in their daily life in the
> family, at work and in society, the unity of a life
> which finds inspiration and strength in the Gospel
> so that they may come to their full completion.[10]

In other words, the life of the new evangelization must
provide space for the world of the laity in all its dimensions
and in the complexity of its activities so that the places that
only lay people can reach may be challenged positively by
their presence. It is obvious that the action undertaken will
be all the more effective the more they are able to bring with
them the community to which they belong, which encour-
ages them in their mission, sustains them in their difficulties
and remains as their place of reference where they may be
able to recount the wonders the Lord has done by means
of their apostolate.

## To reach all people

Some have advanced the criticism that, through the new
evangelization, the Church intends to take the road of
proselytism. As often happens with terms, this one too, over
the course of the centuries, has acquired a negative connotation. This is entirely unjustified, just as the refusal of the
term 'apologetics' on the part of some people, just because
it is identified with a school of thought from a particular
period of history, seems equally unfounded. Since language
lives by means of the use that we make of it, it is obvious
that these terms have fallen into disuse because of the lack
of accurate knowledge of their meaning or because of the
negative dimensions that they have assumed in the course
of recent decades. As far as 'proselytism' is concerned, its
origin is uncertain, but it derives from the Greek prefix *pros*,
joined to the verb *erkomai*; its meaning is that of drawing
closer to something or to someone, 'to approach', 'to go
towards someone' ..., in fact, the basic meaning of the term
is entirely innocent. In a more strictly religious context, it

means to draw close to someone to allow us to share with them our faith, so that they may adhere to it.

Every religion as such requires of its adherents to be proselytes, because it considers it has the right response to the human desire to enter into relationship with God. Without the work of proselytism, religions would become sterile and, therefore, destined to disappear. With all the more reason Christianity, which has an explicit command of the Lord to bring to all people the good news of his proclamation has acted in this way. In the course of recent decades, since some people have misunderstood the meaning of mission, as if it ought no longer to have any place or as if we ought to put an end to any proclamation of the faith, the term has fallen into disuse and has been substituted by 'apostolate' or 'evangelization'. The terms may change, but not their meaning. As has been said a number of times, the Church has the task of evangelising, the mission of sharing the Gospel with all is not for her something *optional*, but it is a command. If she ceased to be the mediatrix of the revelation of Jesus Christ in the world, she would abdicate her very nature and would be destined for insignificance, apart from betraying what the Lord has command her to do.

Hence, the new evangelization is nothing other than the continuing fulfilment of what the Church has done in the last two thousand years, with different methods, but with the same identical purpose, that of announcing Jesus Christ, true God and true man, ultimate and definitive response to the question posed by man of being able to meet God. In him, in fact, it is no longer only man who seeks God, as in the other religions, but it is God who comes to meet human beings once and for all and who offers them the possibility of a love without parallel. The new evangelization, then, is directed in the first instance to Christians, asking them to consider seriously their baptism in terms of an active commitment, consistent with their profession of faith. It is not, therefore, a question of proselytism, which as such is licit, but of a challenge to be Christians in a real sense, assuming the responsibility of growing together to build a better world.

However, if some people are still sceptical about our intentions, they may find in these authoritative statements of Benedict XVI an even more convincing expression. When he was being interviewed by journalists, as is now traditional, on the aeroplane to London on 16th September, 2010, he gave this answer:

> A Church which seeks above all to be attractive would already be on the wrong road. Since the Church does not work for herself, she does not work to increase her own numbers and thereby to increase her own power. The Church is at the service of an Other; she serves not herself to be a strong body, but she serves to render accessible the proclamation of Jesus Christ, the great truths, the great powers of love, of reconciliation, which appeared in him and which always stem from the presence of Jesus Christ, In this sense, the Church does not seek its own attractiveness, but it must be transparent for Jesus Christ. To the extent that she is not wrapped up in herself, as a body which is strong and powerful in this world that seeks her own power, but renders herself simply the voice of an Other, to that extent she becomes truly transparent for the great figure of Jesus Christ and of the great truths that he has brought to us in his humanity.[11]

## Notes

1   Cyril of Jerusalem, *Catecheses*, lecture 22; On the Mysteries IV, n. 3.
2   Augustine, *Speeches*, 340, 1.
3   *Ibid.*, 272, 1.
4   Ignatius of Antioch, *Letter to the Christians at Philadelphia*. IV.
5   Benedict XVI, Homily at the conclusion of the Year of Priests, St Peter's Square, 11th June, 2010.
6   G. Bernanos, *Diary of a Country Priest*, 1937.

7    John Paul II, *Vita consecrata*, n. 45.

8    *Ibid.*, n. 81.

9    Second Vatican Council, *Lumen gentium*, n. 33.

10   John Paul II, *Christifideles laici*, n. 34.

11   Benedict XVI, Interview with journalists on the aeroplane to London, 16th September, 2010.

# CHAPTER 8

# THE WAY OF BEAUTY

## Faith and beauty

It should not be a source of surprise if, within the topic of the new evangelization, we find a place for a reflection on beauty. The *via pulchritudinis* (the way of beauty) belongs in a special way to the mission of proclaiming the Gospel because it is in its very nature to express love through beauty. On the other hand, as the ancient philosophers teach, only that which is beautiful is worthy of being loved. Among the themes of the Sacred Scriptures, moreover, beauty is one of the most preferred; the fact that we may exchange 'beautiful' and 'good' in the same word shows with great clarity the underlying meaning and directs us towards finding unity between the two.

Often we live in a condition which is paradoxical. It appears that the more we refine the meaning of beauty, the more we notice situations of decay and degradation. Our cities reveal the richness of an architectonic genius which over the centuries has brought to realisation works which are unique. We feel very strongly the responsibility for guarding and for transmitting this patrimony to future generations, to make known to them and to share with them this culture of which we are at once the children and the parents.

Nevertheless, at the same time, we can touch with our hands the decadence of the sense of beauty in various expressions of daily life. Unfortunately, it seems that, in some cases, people have wished to impose a model of

beauty in direct discontinuity with tradition, with the result
that we are not allowed to understand the harmony and the
dynamic development that beauty possesses. This is a
serious error because the work of art belongs to what goes
together, to a whole, and wanting to render absolute what
is only a part of this condemns it to the isolation of insignificance. The beauty which has always provoked fascination
and which creates a particular form of contemplation which
impels us towards love seems to be disappearing slowly
from our world, exposing the world to the danger of falling
prey to desperation. If this, regrettably, were to happen, the
emptiness would be enormous and could not be filled by
anything.

Where beauty is in decline, love also comes to be lacking
and, with it, the meaning of life and the capacity to generate.
Unfortunately, our world has over-used the term ('love').
Beauty recurs ever more frequently in our speeches; yet, it
seems that we are no longer capable of looking at it and of
producing it. If, in fact, beauty is limited only to bodiliness
and if it is no longer capable of arousing the genius to affirm
it in works which endure across the years, then it slips into
what is ephemeral and, as a consequence, it loses also its
meaning of truth and goodness. If their power of attraction
is reduced, then we become incapable of creating culture
and, as a consequence, personal and social life become
insipid. This is a risk too great to run, through not seeing
the issues at stake.

The theologian is constantly challenged by the writings
of Hans Urs von Balthasar of half a century ago:

> Beauty is the last word that the thinking intellect can
> dare to pronounce because it does nothing more than
> crown the double star of the true and the good and
> the indissoluble relationship between them. It is
> disinterested beauty, without which the old world
> was incapable of understanding itself and which,
> turning on its heels, has taken its leave of the modern
> world of business, to abandon it to its greed and to
> its sadness. It is the beauty which is no longer loved

nor guarded, not even by religion, the beauty in
which we no longer dare to believe and from which
we have done everything to be able to liberate
ourselves with a lightness of heart.[1]

This is a sad reflection which should shake strongly the
mind of believers so that their responsibility for being
messengers of beauty and for making beauty part of their
message to the world of today may be restored to them. In
fact, from its beginnings Christianity has encountered art.
In the course of the centuries this was for us the favoured
means by which the faith and the good witness we gave
were expressed and represented in a visible manner. In
whatever culture the Gospel of Jesus Christ has been
proclaimed, there voice has been given to beauty, to make
clear the message of the Sacred Scriptures and to show the
reflection of the mystery celebrated in the liturgy. Beauty
has been the best vehicle for communicating the content
proper to our faith; the Gospel is the *beautiful* news of
salvation, brought about by the mystery of the love of Jesus
Christ. Already in the year 406, bishop Paulinus of Nola,
the true fore-runner of the *via pulchritudinis* as a form of
proclaiming Christian truth, could write: 'We have only one
art, the faith; it is Christ, poetry'.[2]

Christianity, unlike other religions, has understood,
though not without considerable effort, that, since the Son
of God had assumed our human nature, it was also possible
to represent it and to show the beauty with which he
clothed it. Art has been placed at the service of this principle
because it understood that every aesthetical path must
necessarily contain within itself the religious as the ultimate
and foundational experience. To sum it up, art expresses
the mystery of the faith better than anything else. The Lord,
in fact, is understood and is celebrated in beauty; not as a
choice of convenience, but as an inescapable necessity to
grasp coherently and fully the mystery which is enclosed
within him. On the other hand, what language could

possibly be able to express better the 'revelation of a mystery kept secret for endless ages' (Rom 16:25)?

Philosophers and poets have competed with one another for primacy, to keep this firm in their hands; yet, the dispute between them did not take into account a third contender, the artist. At one and the same time poet, philosopher and theologian, the artist has been the most coherent artificer of the human language when he has sought to say 'God'. His genius has been able to widen the bars of the cage in which human language is always imprisoned, especially when it takes the path of trying to express what transcends the limits of personal experience. For this reason Christianity has to be in dialogue with art; it cannot allow itself to interrupt a relationship which has been so fruitful because it would deprive itself of a particularly effective means of communicating the foundational message of the faith.

Thus, the mystery is to be joined to beauty or it risks not being able to be perceived in its essence On the other hand, history shows in all its clarity that the relationship between faith and art, apart from being an enviable hendiadys, marks out a path that shows the primacy of beauty. Were the masterpieces of art to be removed from the museums, there would be miles of empty corridors; were sacred music to be removed, we would have tons of empty scores; if we removed from the libraries all the works of Christian literature, we would be left with only a sad sight of dusty shelves. To sum it up, our cathedrals, our churches and a large part of the productive art of almost two millennia are the most effective synthesis and witness to the fruitfulness of the relationship between faith and beauty in the task of transmitting the word of God.

## Safeguarding beauty

'What is beautiful appears to be blessed in itself'.[3] Beauty as such presents itself as a phenomenon which can never be fully determined, even if it remains constantly as an object of speculation. Perhaps, it is the only entity which, maybe because it is not fully capable of being subjected to the laws of rationality, is in a position to break down the barrier of the technical and economic dominion which has been imposed upon us. Why do human beings need beauty? To take up once more the pages of *The Idiot* would not be without its value. Let us recall the dialogue that Dostoyevsky places on the lips of Hippolytus, who, turning to prince Myshkin, ill with consumption and moribund, addresses him in these words:

> Is it true, prince, that once you said that the world would be saved by beauty? My lords – he shouted, speaking unexpectedly to everyone – the prince affirms that the world will be saved by beauty! And I, on the other hand, affirm that he has such frivolous ideas because he is in love. My lords, the prince is in love, I was finally convinced of it as soon as I saw him enter here just now ... What beauty will save the world? ... Are you a fervent Christian? Kolja says that you have taken upon yourself the name of Christian.[4]

Even the atheist, Hippolytus is constrained to inter-relate beauty and love and to refer them to Christianity; to be sure, for him they are 'frivolous ideas', but he himself has no other solution, apart from drowning his days in wine.

Quite rightly, ancient thought could define beauty as *id cuius ipsa apprehensio placet*; that is to say, beauty arouses the peacefulness of contemplation. In the face of beauty, the spirit finds peacefulness and in it finds the refuge to gaze with different eyes upon itself and upon the cosmos which surrounds it.

It was not by accident that St Augustine, driven by his anxieties, was able to write in his *Confessions*: 'Late have I loved you, o Beauty so ancient and so new, late have I loved you! For you were within me and I outside. There I was searching for you!'[5] These are affirmations of a principle to which we should refer; beauty finds a place in our intimate depths, in which there lies truth. We can grasp beauty, in the end, to the extent that the soul perceives the truth and vice versa, we grasp truth when we seek it in its beauty. Once more we return to the requirement to join in unity beauty, truth and goodness as constitutive elements of personal knowledge; without this unity, everything becomes fragmented and devoid of meaning. Beauty, in fact, seeks form and proportion, to allow reality to be expressed in its totality, directing us always beyond the form itself to grasp fully its expressive potential. In a word, beauty allows human beings to love; it seizes them and locates them on a higher level, whence it becomes possible for them to give their whole selves because they understand that, in a definitive way, they have found the response to the meaning of personal existence. In love, in fact, the whole of life is condensed; the tranquillity and the happiness which arise from the contemplation of beauty finally attain their fulfilment.

Giovanni Papini, the controversial Florentine writer of the last century, in his work, *The Last Judgment*, gives expression to two artists who explain their art. The first is Fidia, who, better than anyone else, interprets the principles of the Greek classics, expressing better than anyone else the perfection and the malleability of the forms:

> I was stationary, but I wanted only to model the images of the divinities. I tried in those statues to sublimate the form and the expression of the human figure, to create such perfect examples of humanity, harmonious and serene, that people, looking at them, would have to blush at their own imperfection, decadence and sadness. My statues were designed to teach people a more wonderful reverence for the gods, such as to render them more worthy of those gods and to make them god-like. Thus, they were a continual incitement for human beings to rise above and beyond themselves, to leap beyond the human condition, so as to see themselves in those luminous and noble faces in order to become emulators of the gods.

The second artist, with whom we find ourselves once more in the heart of humanism is Botticelli, who said of himself:

> I spent my whole life designing and painting. The works of my hands were also praised very highly by the people of my time, but no-one, I believe, understood the enormous torment I suffered. Like those who dedicate themselves to art, I was mostly attracted by the exterior beauty of things and of creatures and such love for pretty appearances drew me away, more than I wanted or knew, from the contemplation of divine things and persons. I thought that the true task of the artist consisted of revealing to those who do not see so well the inestimable beauty of the world. This work seemed to me to be such as to foster not only an increase in people's joy, but also in their gratitude towards him who had created so much beauty.[6]

These two examples, even according to the personal understanding of Papino, show the path that art can inspire us to undertake; to raise the soul towards God and to contemplate the beauty of the world, to go beyond that to God. To be sure, to limit ourselves to the natural beauty of the world would be to go astray; still, when there is an expression of beauty, in the end there always opens up before us a path to other realities. The pagan art of Fidia and the Christian art of Botticelli have in common the demand proper to beauty, to draw us beyond the form to enable us to grasp the essence itself that the form contains. In fact, only in this way does contemplation become a way forward to grasp beauty in its original reality deeply and in a way which is coherent. By its very nature, the form which gives expression to beauty does not permit us to remain fixed on itself; it stimulates us to enter into the depths of what it expresses and it draws us beyond to the source itself of beauty, which demands only the silence of contemplation.

## *The cathedral, space for the new evangelization*

Speaking of the beauty of art, a special place is reserved for the cathedral; in fact, very often it is the culminating expression of Christian art. The origin of its beauty can be easily identified in a term which is certainly not foreign to the faith of the Church; rather, it was among the first elements of the content which had to be proclaimed: grace. Aesthetic experience is grace, just as the work which is brought to fruition is grace.

In a cathedral nothing is forgotten, from the foundations to the floor, from the façade to the apse, from the stained-glass windows to the bells …, everything is gathered into the unity of the theological plan to indicate the place where grace is made visible in the sacramental life and where grace itself illuminates and sustains the teaching of the successor of the apostles. Without this reflection, which allows us to grasp the unity and the meaning of the construction, everything would remain as isolated fragments. The faith which supports the edifice, however, allows us to see realised in that space the sense of the sacred, that is to say, the place set apart to lead us to God and to the relationship between him and humanity. To sum it up, the Christian art which takes a concrete form in a cathedral is inspired by what is celebrated and interpreted in that cathedral. The cathedral, in fact, is the special place from which the teaching of the bishop pours out and spreads for his church. As a construction it is an object of his teaching because right to its very stones it declares the function which it is called to fulfil; it is the cathedral from which the pastor gathers his flock to celebrate the blessed Eucharist, the source and summit of the Christian life, and from which stems the ever living proclamation of the understanding of the word of the Lord.[7]

The construction may never be just a simple temple of stones; it expresses the dynamic energies of a community, which in the course of the centuries allows those stones to remain 'living' stones because in them there is expressed the faith of a Church always present in the life of persons and in the history of human beings. Therefore, the liturgical action becomes the key for interpreting and understanding the mystery of faith which is no longer just believed, but which, in this place, is prayed.

The liturgy allows us fully to grasp the beauty of art because it directs us towards that fundamental principle of supreme beauty who became incarnate in the mystery which is celebrated within it. It is not by chance that our Orthodox friends speak of 'earthly paradise' to indicate the liturgy. And so it is. The beauty which exudes from that place is the prelude to that which we believe we shall one day be able to contemplate. In this context the words of St Augustine return to mind in a particularly significant way:

> Brothers, we shall rejoice in a vision never contemplated by any eyes, never heard by any ears, never imagined in any dream, a vision which exceeds all earthly beauties, those of gold, of silver, of woods and of fields, of the sea and of the sky, of the sun and of the moon, of the stars and of the angels. The reason is this; that it is the source of all other beauty.[8]

We should not be amazed, then, if Christians have considered that they must give particular attention to art and if they have invested great resources in it. In the Sacred Scriptures we find described in great detail what must be done to construct works which are destined to proclaim the glory of God. The book of Exodus, when people still found themselves in the middle of the desert, recounts the minute details dedicated to the construction of the ark of the covenant and of the altar and even of the making of priestly vestments.

The wealth of detail in the sacred text is an indication that nothing must be neglected:

> Tell the sons of Israel to set aside a contribution for me; you shall accept this contribution from every man whose heart prompts him to give it You shall accept from them the following contributions: gold,

silver and bronze, purple stuffs of violet shade and
red, crimson stuffs, fine linen, goats' hair, rams'
skins, dyed red, fine leather, acacia wood, oil for the
lamps, spices for the chrism and for the fragrant
incense, onyx stones and gems to be set in ephod
and pectoral. Build me a sanctuary so that I may
dwell among them. In making the tabernacle and its
furnishings, you must follow exactly the pattern I
shall show you. You are to make me an ark of acacia
wood, two and a half cubits long, one and a half
cubits wide, one and a half cubits high. You are to
plate it inside and out with pure gold and decorate
it all around with a gold moulding. You will cast
four gold ring for the ark and fix them to its four
supports, two rings on one side and two rings on the
other. You will also make shafts of acacia wood,
plated with gold (Ex 25:2-13).

No less precise is the description given by the sacred author
of the temple of Solomon; it is enough for us to recall the
provisions for the *sancta sanctorum*:

The twenty cubits measured from the end of the
temple he built of cedar planks, from floor to rafters,
and this part was reserved for the debir, the holy of
holies. The temple measured forty cubits — the hekal —
in front of the debir. There was cedar wood round the
inside of the temple, ornamentally carved with gourds
and rosettes, all was cedar wood, with no stone
showing. In the inner part of the temple he designed
a debir, to contain the ark of the covenant of Yahweh.
The debir was twenty cubits long, twenty cubits wide
and twenty high, and he plated it on the inside with
pure gold. He made an altar of cedar wood in front of
the debir and plated it with gold. He plated the whole
temple with gold, the whole temple, entirely (1 Kg
6:16-22).

All that has been described is not the aseptic inventory of
a construction, but the expression of a faith, which found
in the temple a place where people could be certain that
God dwelt in the midst of his people. In some respects we

ought to be scandalised if Christianity gave less attention to the construction of its churches.

## A *passion for beauty*

Art which is placed at the service of the sacred ought to find us ready to make great sacrifices to produce works which may endure through time to give a witness to the faith. This art, now as in times gone by, ought to express the sense of the unity of the mystery of salvation; from creation to eschatology, passing through the incarnation, everything ought to find a place in contemporary art. The meaning of light, like that of stone, the choice of images and of materials ought to converge to foster the drawing near of believers to the mystery which they are called to celebrate, and not make him feel a stranger in his own house. Christian art ought to be expressed dynamically in a development which is continuous, without breaks and discontinuity with the richness which has preceded us.

I have to admit that it is difficult for me to understand the discontinuity that certain schools of art in the modern and contemporary period have wished to establish with regard to the previous period. I would find it even more incomprehensible to have to recognise this in relation to Christian art. It would be like violence done against our own nature itself, which is called to develop itself dynamically, without any change. On the other hand, if, as the letter to the Hebrews asserts, 'Jesus Christ is the same today as he was yesterday, and as he will be for ever' (Heb 13:8), why should we impose a beauty which is extraneous upon the content to be represented?

Timothy Verdon writes:

> At the beginning of the third millennium, we need to understand who we are, who we were yesterday and who we wish to be tomorrow. At this time of difficult situations, we want to interrogate the past to seek a meaning in history, asking whether there can be continuity between the past and the future.

In a culture such as today's, sensitive to images – or
which entrusts to images the communication of its
more important moral and social messages - the role
of sacred art turns out to be fundamental. Believers
and non-believers remain fascinated by the patrimony of paintings, sculptures and architecture
generated by Christians across the centuries not only
because of the formal beauty of the works, but
because in them they find themselves face to face
with the themes which address the burning questions of today.[9]

When it becomes involved in the sacred and particularly in
Christianity, art bears the great responsibility of giving
voice to the first day and the eighth day; from creation until
the end of time, the beauty which comes from art must be
capable of speaking of the mystery which was accom-
plished on those days and of becoming for everyone a
reminder of the expectation of meeting, a meeting which
will be beautiful because our gaze will meet that of original
beauty itself. Hence, the wealth of sacred art becomes the
interpreter of the history of salvation and of the anticipation
of its happiness .

Very rightly did Joseph Ratzinger write: 'Sacred art finds
its contents in the images of the history of salvation,
beginning from creation and from the first day up to the
eighth day, the day of the resurrection, and of the return in
which the line of history is completed'; for this reason

the complete absence of images is not compatible
with faith in the incarnation of God. In his action in
history God has entered into our world of the senses,
so that that world may become transparent with
respect to him. The images of beauty, in which the
mystery of the invisible God is rendered visible,
belong to the cult of Christians. To be sure, there will
also be an up and a down in the course of time, a
rising and a decline; therefore, there will also be
times in which there is a certain poverty of images.

> But they cannot ever be lacking altogether. Icono-
> clasm is not a option for Christians.[10]

Here, then, is another indication to place Christian art in its proper niche as an experience of the new evangelization. We must be able to let our works of art speak because they were born with the purpose of making known the beautiful news brought by Jesus Christ. We have art treasures which constitute an authentic catechism for our time. I am thinking of what great power for evangelization we will be able to unleash if we can succeed in providing a clear explanation, adhering to the faith, of our cathedrals, our churches and our sanctuaries. The new evangelization passes also by this route; rather, in some cases, it is the first proclamation which reaches those who have become distant from their faith. The need to form real experts as guides to these masterpieces cannot be put off any longer. Joining the study of art to the knowledge of the contents of the faith will be obligatory if we want our works of art to remain instruments capable of provoking reflection and of expressing how the faith of *yesterday* is possible also for our contemporaries.

In a period in which it appears that beauty is only a matter of mere desire, because it is obscured by works of an ambiguous nature, the need to encounter true artists returns all the more forcefully. Thus, the words addressed by the Second Vatican Council to artists acquire particular significance:

> Now, all you artists, enamoured of beauty, and who
> have worked for her, poets, men of letters, painters,
> sculptors, architects, musicians, those in the theatre
> and the cinema … To all of you, the Church of the
> Council says by means of our voice: if you are
> friends of true art, you are our friends. A long time
> ago the Church made a covenant with you. You have
> built and decorated her churches, celebrated her
> dogmas, enriched her liturgy. You have helped her
> to translate her divine message into the language of

forms and figures, to make the invisible world comprehensible. Today, as yesterday, the Church needs you and turns to you. She tells you by means of our voice: do not let us break a covenant which has been so fruitful! Do not refuse to place your talent at the service of divine truth! Do not close off your spirit from the breath of the Holy Spirit! This world in which we live needs beauty so as not to collapse into desperation. Beauty, like truth, is that which pours joy into people's hearts, it is that precious fruit which resists the weariness of time, which unites generations and which makes it possible to communicate with them in wonder. And this is thanks to your hands … May those hands remain pure and disinterested! Remember that you are the custodians of beauty in the world; this should be enough to free you from passing tastes without real value, to free you from seeking expressions which are excessive or in poor taste. Always and everywhere, be worthy of your ideals.[11]

In all probability, this will be possible if we care capable of proclaiming the beauty of faith in Jesus Christ; only in this way, in fact, will the power of the proclamation be a stimulus to the intelligence and the sensitivity of the artist. The faith, then, will still be able to give rise to works capable of leading us to contemplation, to restore the joy and the serenity of an encounter with beauty. Beauty does not fade away, but it needs persons who are able every day of rejuvenating its face, conscious that that cathedral is not made of stones, but of men and women who, by their faith, wish still in our days to proclaim the beauty of the face of Jesus of Nazareth, true God and true man, the final answer to the quest for meaning of our contemporaries.

## Notes

1    H. U, von Balthasar, *The Glory of the Lord: A Theological Aesthetics* (1989), vol I, p. 10.
2    Paulinus of Nola, *Carmen*, 20, 32.

3    'Was aber schön ist, selig scheint es in ihm selber', in E Moerike, *Idylie vom Bodensee oder Fischer Martin*, 1846.

4    F. Dostoyevsky, *The Idiot*, part III, ch. V.

5    Augustine, *Confessions*, 10, 27, 38.

6    G. Papini, *Giudizio universale* (Firenze: 1957), pp. 861-862, 872-874, cited by C. Valenziano, *Bellezza del Dio di Gesù Cristo* (Gorle: 2000), p. 10.

7    Cf. J. Doré, 'Un livre de référence de la cathédrale de Strasbourg' in *La grâce d'une cathédrale* (Strasbourg: 2007), p. 7.

8    Augustine, *Commentary on the First Letter of St John*, 4: 5.

9    T. Verdon, *L'arte cristiana in Italia* (Cinisello Balsamo, Milano, 2006), p. 27.

10   J. Ratzinger, *Teologia della liturgia, Opera omnia*, vol XI (Città del Vaticano: 2010), p. 129

11   Paul VI, *Message to artists* (8 December 1965), at the end of the Second Vatican Council.

# CHAPTER 9

# THE ICON

## A wonderful intuition

The Sagrada Familia (Holy Family) of Gaudí, consecrated by Benedict XVI in Barcelona on 17th November 2010, can be taken as the icon of the new evangelization. Relating the history of this church may help us to understand the reason for this choice and what significant elements can be traced there to foster a pastoral action capable of representing the riches of the Gospel and the contribution of the Church to the growth and to the development of culture. The Sagrada Familia today is known all over the world. When they thought of building the church, though, the basic idea was never to make of it an iconic temple of a new relationship between the Church and the world, and no-one would ever have dreamt of making this its objective. Certainly, it was a wonderful intuition, but it was limited to the social, political and cultural realty of the end of the nineteenth century, which then characterised the lively city of Barcelona. It was the period in which the Catalan population, at all levels, was recovering more and more its own identity under the stimulus of the industrial revolution. The spiritual power which permeated all sectors of society became the motive force of a movement which would rediscover not only a strong social identity, but also a strong sense of belonging.

It was in this scenario that the idea of the owner of an old religious bookshop of the city, Josep Maria Bocabella i Verdaguer, arose of building a church in honour of Saint Joseph, financed by his personal generosity and that of all the faithful who would wish to contribute to it. Thus, no-one from the hierarchy took the initiative for the construction, as normally would happen, but it was the fruit of popular sentiment which, as was written on the parchment preserved in the foundation stone, had the a purpose of 'Re-awakening from their torpor hearts grown drowsy. To exalt the faith. To grant warmth to charity. To offer to reverence for the Lord from the country.' These few indications are sufficient to point out to us the way we are called to go, if we are to understand its symbolic significance for our times. To re-awaken many people who have distanced themselves from the Church is an urgent task for Christians, who must stay awake to recognise the presence of the Lord who brings us joy.

According to Bocabella's intention the church was to have expressed the deep meaning of the value of Christ's redemption. Just at the time of the expansion of the city, he wanted the Sagrada Familia to be a clear sign that the Church could not be extraneous to the development of Barcelona; quite the opposite, where the city was growing, there the presence of the Church needed to be evident. Thus it was that in the area of the Eixample in 1881 the land on which the church would be constructed was acquired for 172,000 pesetas, little more than 1000 euros at present. On the feast of St Joseph in the following year the first stone was laid, with the initial project of reproducing there the church of Loreto, where, according to tradition, the house of Nazareth is preserved. Somehow, everything seemed to be being put together happily, but a serious difficulty presented itself already in the very early years. The project was becoming very demanding in the face of a lack of finances. In place of Francisco de Villar, the first director of the project, there came Antonio Gaudí, a young architect of only 31 years of age, who, in a short time by means of his personal genius, revolutionised the initial project, transforming the Sagrada Familia into the masterpiece we admire today. His intention had no lack of great idealism nor of positive ambition. Gaudí wanted to unite mysticism and art; that is to say, something that would speak intuitively of the faith, and not a single stone of the building was to be deprived of this reference.

The Sagrada Familia was to be the place where prayer would become the first thought for all those who entered it and the discovery of the transcendent would accompany the path trod by all who raised their gaze upon its interior. One of his writings indicates this explicitly:

> These inscriptions will be like a helical band which will rise to the towers. All those who read them, even the incredulous, will intone the hymn to the Blessed Trinity, as little by little they uncover its content; the *Sanctus, Sanctus, Sanctus,* which, while they read it, will guide their gaze towards heaven.[1]

And this was possible because Gaudí lived a profound experience of the faith. Prompted by the desire to give life to something truly original and extra-ordinary, but in continuity with the tradition, the architect formed himself in the school of theology, studied liturgy and infused every stone of the church with the history of salvation in the same way as did the old Gothic cathedrals of the Middle Ages, true Bibles of stone. We can become aware, tangibly, of his faith, ever more intense and profound, by observing the structure itself of the church, which we think it will be useful to describe in more detail.

## A catechism in stone

The first façade to be constructed was that of the Nativity. The mystery of the incarnation of God constitutes the culminating point of the religious phenomenon and the originality proper to the Christian faith. It was not by chance that Gaudí wanted to adorn the façade with three porticos dedicated to the three theological virtues, respectively placed under the protection of the three persons of the Holy Family. The central portico, in fact, the highest, is dedicated to charity and sees Jesus as the culminating expression of the love of God. It is constructed as if it were a great grotto in memory of the facts of Bethlehem and there is a beautiful exhibition of different representations of the crib, from the shepherds to the magi. In the account of the birth, the child Jesus is protected by Mary and Joseph, while the dividing column furnishes the entire genealogy of Jesus, to reaffirm his presence in history and his being rooted in the Jewish people.

The second portico represents faith, whose exemplary icon is Mary. The principal scenes from the infancy and adolescence of Jesus are represented here: in the arms of the old man, Simeon, when he was speaking to the doctors in the temple, and when he was learning the work of a carpenter; Mary, however, emerges in the statue of the Immaculate Conception as the most significant expression of this portico. The third represents hope and finds in St Joseph its most vivid example.

In these porticos Gaudí wanted also to insert the entire creation, as it renders glory to God for the mystery of the birth of his Son. Mounted here and there it is possible to see the different species of animals who, as in the canticle of the three young men in the book of Daniel and subsequently in the *Canticle of the Creatures* of Saint Francis, are all called to bless the Lord. The idea is not foreign to the ancient cathedrals and in any case the representation of the various animals makes a great impression, since, apart from their symbolic effect, they often have the value of keeping evil at a distance. In his own way Gaudí takes up the symbolism of those we known in daily life. Of all of them, I am struck most especially by the symbolism of the tortoise placed at the base of the columns. The image is clear; the foundation of everything is constituted by the faith. In the course of the centuries its fundamental contents remain unchanged and yet it is not static; its slow, but progressive, pace advances with an irreducible constancy and comes to a good end. Finally, the most spectacular pinnacle of the façade seeks in some way to be the synthesis of all the themes treated in the porticos and so here is the presence of the tree of life, which, in the vision of the Apocalypse, remains forever green and bears fruits and whose leaves are used to heal the nations (Apoc 22:2). At the top, the representation of the Trinity, which will find its greatest splendour in the façade of glory, shows how this inexhaustible mystery of faith is the source and the highest point of the life of the believer and, at the same time, the end to which it tends because it invites us to participate in the Trinitarian love of God.

The façade of the passion immediately provokes a sensation of grief and of sadness. The sculpture of Josip Maria Subirachs, who interprets personally the studies left by Gaudí, are hard and stylised; they lack the decoration of the other porticos and everything is tense, to accentuate the dramatic nature of the events which lead to the death of Jesus. The word, in this case, is left to the very hardness of the stone and to its bareness. The inclining columns, similar to tree trunks and in the form of bones, contribute to increasing the sense of desolation in the narrative. From the last supper until the crucifixion, the scenes described go back over the facts of the passion in succession in such a way as to show the path trod by Jesus on the way to Golgotha. The armour of the Roman soldiers, the serpent who inspires treachery in Judas, Malchus' severed ear, Peter asleep in the garden, find their synthesis in the cryptogram of sixteen numbers, the modern cabala. The sum of 310 possible combinations of the 16 numbers is always and only 33, which tradition records as Christ's age.

If the portico of the nativity intends to celebrate the mystery of the incarnation of the Son of God, the façade of glory honours the mystery *par excellence* of the faith, represented by the Blessed Trinity, and at the same time constitutes a hymn of praise to the divinity of Jesus Christ. Precisely for this reason, Gaudí conceived it in great luminosity, in harmony with the words of Jesus which invite us to be light to the world (Jn 8:12).

The Catalan architect only had time to sketch out this façade; yet, even from the notes there emerges the message he wanted to leave. Here we discover again a real catechism where, from creation to the last judgment, the path is pointed out towards the fulfilment in eternal life. The profession of faith, the Our Father, the sacraments, paradise and hell ..., in fact everything seems to be configured to show the climax of the life which will never have an end. At the centre appears the glorious Christ, not deprived of the marks of the passion, but now surrounded by angels in the act of undertaking the final judgment, as the culminating moment of his glory, acquired by his death out of love.

The Sagrada Familia, with its towers and spires, which seem to touch heaven, obliges us to look upwards. In some respects, the intention which drove Gaudí was no different from that which guided the construction of the medieval cloisters. All those who walked there could only see the sky; nothing and no-one was to block the sky-line, as it was marked out by the cloister. In this case too, whoever wants to admire the beauty of the construction has to force himself to gaze on high, where the mystery of our own existence finds its full meaning. On the other hand, no-one can conceive of their own life enclosed only within spatio-temporal categories. There is something which urges us to go further, which compels us towards the sense of the transcendent which is perceived in our depths and which traces its essential path, to enable us to decipher the enigmas of our condition as human persons.

The words of the French philosopher, Maurice Blondel, are no more than a truthful echo of this existential experience: 'There is an element of the infinite present in all our voluntary acts and this element of the infinite we cannot contain for ourselves within our reflections, nor can we reproduce it by our own human efforts'.[2] The highest tower of the Sagrada Familia will be dedicated to Christ; its height of 170 metres, which will make it one of the highest in the world, represents the meeting we need with the Son of God, in which the human puzzle will be resolved and man's demand for meaning will find its fulfilment. The towers of the apostles and that of the Virgin Mary act as a crown, indicating the one upon whom we really ought to fix our gaze.

Anyone who, with an attentive eye, admires Gaudí's architectonic work, pregnant with meaning, will find the voices of yesterday and those of today. It can escape no-one that it is a church, a sacred space, that cannot be confused with any other construction. Its spires stand out, pointing on high, obliging us to look up to the sky. Its pillars have no Corinthian or Ionic capitals and yet they recall these, but surpass them, running into a woven pattern of arches which makes us think of a forest in which the mystery invades you and, far from being oppressive, offers you serenity instead. The beauty of the Sagrada Familia knows how to speak to people of today, while retaining the strong features of ancient art. Gaudí's genius has been to be able to unite, in a way which is both intelligent and original, the faith and art in a dynamic of development which does not alter the contents of either. Everyone recognises the Gothic traits of the church, but no-one can deny that that style is expressed according to the new spirit of the time. The vertical structure impressed on that church exceeds very greatly that of the Gothic cathedrals, even the most famous of them; for the external bulwarks to sustain the weight Gaudí substitutes tilted and branching columns, so that, notwithstanding their fragility, while creating a kind of game of intersecting labyrinths, they show the way out, which is upwards, ever further upwards, to enter into contact with him who stands above space and time.

## A church for the city

The presence of the Sagrada Familia, today in particular, seems to stand in stark contrast to the metropolis made of buildings and streets, one on top of the other, the icon of modernity of which we are both the artificers and the victims. However, the two realities do not clash with each other. They live one with the other and, in some respects, they seem to be made for each other, the church for the city and vice versa. Gaudí's idea has been confirmed and Bocabella's wish has become a reality. His fundamental intuition has been realised in visible form; where the city expands, there too is found the meaningful presence of the Church. Today it is clear that the city, without that church, would be deprived of something essential; if there were no Sagrada Familia, the only thing that would appear clearly would be a void, that no casting of cement could fill. Gaudí liked to say: 'The building of the Sagrada Familia is slow because the Patron of this work is not in a hurry'. So indeed it seems. The Lord of all, who took seven days to complete the first creation, now awaits its completion according to his timetable, and not ours.

Perhaps in this context the words of St Ambrose may still be significant. Commenting upon creation, the bishop of Milan wanted to do so in the light of beauty; in certain respects, some of his expressions may recall the rhythms imposed by Gaudí in his time: 'God first created things; then he made them beautiful.'[3] 'As those who sculpture out of marble human faces and human bodies or model them in bronze or reproduce them in wax ...',[4] so God every day places into all that he has created a beauty such that it will be able to be contemplated in its completeness only once creation is finished. Creation brings with it harmony and everything is made to be in concord with other things; in fact, a supreme intelligence who composes a work of art. A real 'masterpiece', Ambrose writes, which culminates in the creation of the human being 'the highest beauty of every created being'.[5]

To the reader who is distracted it could appear that everything is resolved with Adam, but this is not so. Ambrose is too attentive, speculative and a man of contemplation to forget the real step forward to which beauty leads.

On the same wavelength are the words of Pope Benedict XVI on the day of the consecration of Gaudí's church:

> In the heart of the world, before the gaze of God and
> of humanity, in a humble and joyous act of faith, we
> have erected an immense mass of material, the fruit
> of the nature of an incalculable effort of the human
> intelligence which constructed this work of art. It is
> a visible sign of the invisible God, to whose glory
> these towers rise up, arrows which point out the
> absolute of light and he who is Light, Height and
> Beauty itself. [6]

The Sagrada Familia is not finished. We shall need a long
period of time yet before that the church may be completed
according to the plan of its architect. This component too
belongs to the Church's work of new evangelization. This
continues with much effort, becoming strong only on the
basis of human weakness, knowing that the real builder is
the Spirit of Christ, who leads her along paths he has chosen
that she should tread. Yet, precisely through this work of
dynamic development, evangelization comes to be
expressed in a way which is capable of reaching people of
every age. It cannot block itself in the past, but it needs to
follow human beings along the path of the continual
becoming of history. In this history God has become
incarnate and it is of this history that the proclamation of
the Gospel announces him to be the Lord and Redeemer.
As the Sagrada Familia was constructed with the offerings
of the people, so the new evangelization expects the offering
of every believer, who may place his or her life at the service
of the Gospel, to make people of today more aware of their
calling to an existence which is better and less superficial.

In conclusion, I think it may be useful to make a last
appeal to the symbolic value of the Sagrada Familia for the
new evangelization, which is connected to the very name
of Gaudí's work, the family. One of the fundamental
contents to which the new evangelization must commit
itself is certainly the centrality of the family, not only for
the life of the Church, but also for society itself. The
Christian community understands its fundamental value
in the transmission of the faith. The family, in fact, is the

cell on which the community is sustained; itself a community, it is a sacramental sign of the reciprocity of love and makes evident the relationship of love which binds the Lord Jesus to his Church (cf. Eph 5:23–32). The family is the beating heart where the call to life begins and it expresses, in an analogy, the mystery of love which never fades.

Society is living through an experience which is highly paradoxical in regard to the family. While its irreplaceable role is recognised in theory, in its reality it seems to be continually being torn apart and broken down. Policies which are designed to increase alternative models, legal recognition of forms of cohabitation which cannot be considered to be family under any rubric, the lack of attention to social support, linked to other legislative choices and administrative decisions, relegate it to a secondary level, perpetrating thereby a very real attack upon its centrality for the value of life and for the structure of society.

The Church was described by John Paul II as a 'family of families', a new image that came to be joined to the classical images of Sacred Scripture and which shows the tireless journey she is called to undertake to make herself understood by her contemporaries. From this perspective, too, the Sagrada Familia becomes an icon of art which deserves to be contemplated and of the contents of faith which need to be proclaimed and known.

## Notes

[1]   Cited by L. Martinez Sistach, 'Segno di Dio nel cuore della metropoli' in *L'Osservatore Romano* (1 June 2011).

[2]   M. Blondel, *L'action 1893*, (Paris: 1973), p. 418.

[3]   Ambrose, *Hexameron*, , II, 7, 27.

[4]   *Ibid.*, III, 5, 21.

[5]   *Ibid.*, IX, 10, 75.

[6]   Benedict XVI, *Homily at the consecration of the Sagrada Familia* (7 November 2010).

# Chapter 10

## Concluding synthesis

### A journey of two thousand years

I consider that this book does not need a conclusion. It is better to leave the reflection open to the reactions it may provoke and to future contributions. It is better, therefore, to provide a synthesis in which the main features of the preceding pages are resumed. In the speech directed to the cardinals and bishops, members of the Pontifical Council for the Promotion of the New Evangelization, at the time of their first meeting on 30th May 2011, Benedict XVI said:

> The term 'new evangelization' recalls the need for a renewed way of proclamation, especially for those who live in a context, such as the present one, in which the development of secularisation has left its heavy mark, even in countries of Christian tradition. The Gospel is the proclamation, ever new, of the salvation effected by Christ to make human beings sharers in the mystery of God and of his life of love and to open to them a future of hope, which is reliable and strong. To underline the fact that the Church is called in this time to undertake a *new* evangelization means to intensify her missionary action in order to respond fully to the Lord's command.[1]

As is known, the new evangelization requires the capacity to be able to provide reasons for our own faith, showing Jesus Christ, the Son of God, the only saviour of humanity. To the extent that we are able to do this, we shall be able to offer our contemporaries the answer they seek and that we have to put forward to them.

Continuing his discourse, the Pope added:

To proclaim Jesus Christ the only saviour of the world, today appears to be more complex than in the past, but our task remains the same as it was at the dawn of our history. The mission has not changed, just as the enthusiasm and the courage which motivated the apostles must not change. The Holy Spirit who pressed them to open the doors of the upper room, making them evangelizers (cf. Acts 2:1-4), is the same Spirit who moves the Church to make a renewed proclamation of hope to the people of our time. St Augustine states that we must not think that the grace of evangelization was extended to the apostles and that, with them, this source of grace was exhausted, but 'that source becomes clear when it is flowing, not when it has ceased to flow. And it was in such a way that grace, through the apostles, reached others too, who were sent out to proclaim the Gospel ... rather, it has continued to call people up to these last days, the entire body of his Only Son, that is his Church, spread throughout the world.'

The grace of the mission always needs new evangelizers, capable of accepting it so that the proclamation of the word of God may not fall behind in the changing conditions of history ... There exists a dynamic continuity between the proclamation of the first apostles and our own. In the course of the centuries the Church has never ceased proclaiming the salvific mystery of the death and resurrection of Jesus Christ, but this same proclamation today needs a renewed vigour to convince contemporary people, often distracted and insensitive. For this reason, the new evangelization will have to take on the task of finding the ways to make the proclamation of salvation more effective, without which personal existence remains in its state of contradiction and deprived of what is essential. Even in respect of those who remain attached to their Christian roots, but who are living through a difficult relationship with modernity, it is important to help them to understand that being a Christian is not a kind of garment to be worn in private or on particular occasions, but is something alive and all-embracing.[2]

In other words, says the Pope, the path of the new evangelization is none other than the continuing journey which, from the apostles, has come to us across twenty centuries of history. It must be lived out under the primacy of grace, which allows everyone to perceive the living presence of the Holy Spirit who transforms our hearts and who allows us to welcome the message of salvation.

## Firm in faith

The words of the apostle, Paul, may also be a warning to the new evangelizers:

> You must lead your whole life according to the Christ you have received—Jesus the Lord; you just be rooted in him and built on him and held firm by the faith you have been taught and full of thanksgiving. Make sure that no-one traps you and deprives you of your freedom by some second-hand, empty, rational philosophy based on the principles of this world instead of on Christ (Col 2:6–8).

The condition of the Christian community today is not very different from that of the first disciples in the city of Colossae. Contrary to Christians from other communities, the life and the behaviour of these believers did not give Paul any reason to complain. The news he received was worthy of praise both for their faith in Jesus Christ and in regard to their witness of charity; both one and the other pervaded their thoughts and were a support for their hope, as the words at the beginning of the letter enable us to see:

> We have never failed to remember you in our prayers and to give thanks for you to God, the Father of our Lord, Jesus Christ, ever since we heard about your faith in Christ Jesus and the love that you show to all the saints because of the hope which is stored up for you in heaven. It is only recently that you

heard of this when it was announced in the message
of the truth (Col 1:3–5).

Nevertheless, the Apostle's concern is directed to the cultural
context within which the believers were living. He felt that
they might easily be deceived by false doctrines, by false
philosophies which lay outside of his preaching, by false
ideas which might lead them to eliminate the novelty of the
Gospel. The invitation put forward to Christians, therefore,
is that of being able to discern between what is true and what
is false, between that which can be fruitful and that which,
on the other hand, is sterile and ephemeral.

It is interesting to note that Paul reminds the Colossians
that the first point is their profession of the faith. Christ had
been proclaimed to them; they had heard his word, had
accepted the Gospel and had been converted. They had
built their life upon this combined basis, together with a
way of conduct such as to make them recognisable as
disciples of the Lord. Hence, the community was to remain
firmly rooted in the proclamation made by the apostle,
without any breaking away from it.

To sum it up, the transmission of the faith is decisive,
because on that basis both fidelity to the Gospel and the
open-hearted welcoming of those who come to faith are
determined. The four expressions to which Paul makes
reference are particularly interesting and remain also for us
as imperatives: 'to be rooted in the Lord', 'to be firm in the
faith', 'to be full of thanksgiving' and 'to take care no-one
deceives you'.

The solidity of the rock on which Christian existence is
built is not in contradiction to the path they are constantly
called to follow to penetrate more deeply into the mystery.
Planting and growing, moreover, are cause and effect and
only in this way is it possible to build up the community
ever anew with more disciples. In the same way, this
solidity is reinforced by the teaching which is offered to
Christians, so that they may not be jolted by all sorts of
visions of life. The call to vigilance, so that no-one is left

trapped, is a real worry for the apostle, not only so that his ministry would not have been in vain, but especially so that Christians would not fall back into a situation in which life had no sense for them.

The thanksgiving, therefore, makes it possible to confirm the extent to which the life of the Christian community finds its deepest and irreplaceable locus of meaning in prayer. It is not a question only of giving thanks to the Lord with hymns and canticles proper to prayer, but of experiencing the time of the liturgical action to the full measure which is due to it for the gift of faith received. In a word, the apostle places believers once more before the fullness of the life of faith, which is expressed in the credo, in prayer and in witness.

## Building together

In our time too, as was done in times past, we need to face up to the difficulties which confront us. As in the past, this gave rise to an intense activity of evangelization, so also today the Church needs to become aware of the great commitment which the new evangelization demands. The words of St Augustine may come to our support, when he writes:

> Who are those who work to build up the Church? All those who in the Church preach the word of God, the ministers of God's sacraments. We are all in the race, we are all making the effort, now we are all involved in the building. And, prior to us, others have been involved in the race, others have struggled, others have built. But, 'if the Lord does not build the house, those who build labour in vain' . For this reason there was no lack of warnings from the apostles who saw some people behaving badly and, in particular, the voice of Paul resounds, when he says: 'You and your special days and months and seasons and years! You make me feel I have wasted my time with you' (Gal 4:10–11). Since he was aware that the Church was built up interiorly by the Lord,

he felt sorry for these people because he had
laboured in vain among them, without there being
an appropriate response. Thus, we speak from the
outside; Christ builds from within. We may be able
to see what attention you give, but what you are
thinking only he who sees your thoughts knows...
It is he who builds, who warns, who instils fear, who
opens up the mind, who directs your mind to the
faith And yet, we too labour as his workers.[3]

As has been noted, it needs to be repeated once more that
the new evangelization needs to entrust itself to God, who
shows us the paths to follow, and to the support of the Holy
Spirit, who precedes, guides and sustains the new evangelizers.

In this context, it is worth recalling a story from the
Middle Ages. A poet passed by some work being conducted
and saw three workers busy at their work; they were stone
cutters. He turned to the first and said: 'What are you doing,
my friend?' This man, quite indifferently, replied: 'I am
cutting a stone'. He went a little further, saw the second and
posed to him the same question, and this man replied,
surprised: 'I am involved in the building of a column'. A
bit further ahead, the pilgrim saw the third and to this man
to he put the same question; the response, full of enthusiasm, was: 'I am building a cathedral'.

The old meaning is not changed by the new work we are
called to construct. There are various workers called into
the vineyard of the Lord to bring about the new evangelization; all of them will have some reason to offer to explain
their commitment. What I wish for and what I would like
to hear is that, in response to the question: 'What are you
doing, my friend?', each one would be able to reply: 'I am
building a cathedral'. Every believer who, faithful to his
baptism, commits himself or herself with effort and with
enthusiasm every day to give witness to their own faith
offers their original and unique contribution to the construction of their great cathedral in the world of today. It is the
Church of our Lord, Jesus, his body and his spouse, the

people constantly on the way without ever becoming weary, which proclaims to all that Jesus is risen, has come back to life, and that all who believe in him will share in his own mystery of love, the dawn of a day which is always new and which will never fade.

I have recalled this in the expressive words of Benedict XVI in his homily on Corpus Christi, 2011, almost sketching out a method of work:

> There is nothing magic in Christianity. There are no short cuts, but everything passes through the humble, patient logic of the grain of wheat which dies to give life, the logic of the faith which moves mountains with the meek strength of God. For this reason God wishes to renew humanity, its history and the universe by means of this chain of transformations of which the Eucharist is the sacrament. By means of the consecrated bread and wine, in which his Body and Blood are truly present, Christ transforms us, assimilating us to himself; he involves us in his work of redemption, making us capable by means of the grace of the Holy Spirit of living according to the same logic which is his, that of gift, like grains of wheat united to Him and in Him. Thus, sown and maturing in the furrows of history are the unity and peace which are the end to which we are directed, according to the plan of God. Without any illusions, without ideological utopias, we pass along the roads of the world, bearing within ourselves the Body of the Lord, as did the Virgin Mary in the mystery of the Visitation. With the humility of recognising ourselves as simple grains of wheat, we preserve the firm certitude that the love of God, incarnate in Christ, is more powerful than evil, than violence and than death. We know that God has prepared for all people a new heavens and a new earth, in which peace and justice will reign – and in faith we glimpse the new world, which is our real fatherland. This evening, too, we set off on a journey; with us there is Jesus in the Eucharist, the Risen One

who has said: 'I am with you always, even to the end of the world' (Mt 28:20).

A few days before being elected as Pope, Benedict XVI had delivered a lecture at Subiaco on the condition of Europe. In his lucid analysis of the present time, he expressed himself, amongst other things, in these far-sighted words, which constitute a programme for the new evangelizers:

> What we need at this time of history are people, who, through a faith which is enlightened and lived out in practice, make God credible in this world … We need people who keep their gaze fixed upon God, learning from there what true humanity is. We need people whose intellect is enlightened by the light of God and whose hearts God may open up in such a way that their intellect may speak to the intellect of others and that their hearts may open the hearts of others. Only through people who are touched by God can God return to humanity.[4]

Hence, the new evangelization starts from here: from the credibility of our living as believers and from the conviction that grace acts and transforms to the point of converting the heart. It is a journey which still finds Christians committed to it after two thousand years of history.

## Notes

[1]  Pope Benedict XVI, *Discourse to the members of the Pontifical Council for the Promotion of the New Evangelization* (30 May 2011).

[2]  *Ibid.*, see Augustine, *Sermon* 239.1.

[3]  Augustine, *Commentary on the Psalms*, Ps 126:2.

[4]  J. Ratzinger, Cardinal Ratzinger on 'Europe's Crisis of Culture', (www.zenith.org 2005), translation of *L'Europa di Benedetto nella crisis della cultura* (Siena: 2005), pp. 63–64.

Lightning Source UK Ltd.
Milton Keynes UK
UKOW050946300812

198230UK00001B/8/P